GRANDMA

GRANDMA
The Biography of Giles's Infamous Cartoon Character

Robert Beaumont

Introduction by Rosie Boycott

HEADLINE

To Claire, David and Emma

First published in 1999 by HEADLINE BOOK PUBLISHING

10 9 8 7 6 5 4 3 2 1

British Library Cataloguing in Publication Data
Beaumont, Robert
Grandma
1.English wit and humor, Pictorial
I.Title
741.5'941

ISBN 0 7472 7497 5

Typeset by Letterpart Limited, Reigate, Surrey
Designed by John Hawkins
Printed and bound in Italy by Canale & C.S.p.A.

HEADLINE BOOK PUBLISHING
A division of the Hodder Headline Group
338 Euston Road
London NW1 3BH
www.headline.co.uk
www.hodderheadline.com

Contents

Acknowledgements

Could I thank the following for their invaluable kindness, interest and help during the writing of *Grandma*: David Nicholson, David and Kate Paul, Suzanne Savill, Sue McGeever and Mark Burgess of Express Newspapers, Nigel Pickover, David Rose of Ipswich Town FC, Paul Gravett of the Cartoon Art Trust, Philip Hope-Cobbold, Valerie Maddison and last, but not least, Rosie Boycott for taking the trouble to write the introduction.

Introduction

I am delighted to have the opportunity to follow in the footsteps of such distinguished *Express* editors as John Gordon, Sir John Junor and Sir Alastair Burnett and write an introduction to a book celebrating the life and work of Giles.

Carl Giles was not only a great cartoonist, but he was also a mainstay of the *Daily* and the *Sunday Express* for 40 years. In some ways Giles was a square peg in a round hole, because he was a lifelong socialist writing for what were then essentially conservative newspapers. But he felt at home at Express Newspapers – and his cartoons cut right across the political and social divide to speak to the British man and woman in the street. It is ironic, since Giles was a self-confessed chauvinist, that his main mouthpiece was a woman. And what a woman! His Grandma is one of the most magnificent creations in the history of British cartoons, a multi-dimensional firebrand whose trenchant works and deeds put the fear of God into everyone who crossed her path.

In this book, dedicated to Grandma and her extraordinary life, it is a pleasure to laugh and to cry with her. We see her putting a punk rocker in his place, speaking up for the harassed and dwindling band of smokers, causing havoc in church and mayhem in the doctor's surgery and sinking enough brown ale and whisky to make a grown man weep.

Week in, week out, Giles used Grandma as his mouthpiece to comment on the absurd nature of this mixed-up world. Dressed from head to toe in black, and wielding a dangerous-looking umbrella, Grandma never failed to amuse or to introduce a lighter, brighter perspective on life.

Coincidentally, I have known Robert Beaumont, the author of this entertaining and informative look at Grandma, since we were both children. Little did I think that our paths would cross over Carl Giles, but I am pleased they have. This book has also solved the biggest mystery of all for generations of Giles' fans – Robert's meticulous research has led to the discovery of the real-life model for Grandma. As we approach the millennium, it is appropriate to celebrate the life and times of someone like Grandma who summed up the twentieth century like no one else. Happy reading.

Rosie Boycott
Editor, *The Express*

Chapter One

An appreciation of Giles

There have been many attempts to define the genius of Carl Giles the cartoonist and to understand the character of Carl Giles the man. The two are inextricably linked and are so devilishly complex that most of those attempts to pigeonhole Giles have ended in ignominious failure.

Giles himself was a mass of contradictions, a socialist with a taste for the high life and a grumpy old so-and-so with a heart of gold. His cartoons are more straightforward, but they still defy total analysis. They are, like Giles, unique.

No one has come closer to intuitively understanding Giles than John Gordon, one of the finest editors Fleet Street has ever known. Gordon was the man responsible for bringing Giles to Express Newspapers in 1943 and for giving him the freedom to draw as he wished.

In the introduction to the *Giles Annual* of 1946, now a sought-after collector's item, John Gordon wrote: 'Giles has that greatest of all gifts of genius, the common touch. He knows the common people, their troubles, their foibles, their joys, and their aspirations. He is, in fact, the common man. But he is something more than a great cartoonist. Study his work closely and you will find that he is a great artist as well.

'And, finally, the people in his cartoons, those odd children and those even odder grown-ups. When I looked at them first, I didn't think they were real people. But I was wrong. I know it now. For whenever I pass along the street, I look at the people and think: Giles is right. Every face is a Giles face. Try it for yourself.'

The left-wing author and would-be iconoclast Colin McInnes was much less charitable, accusing Giles of being 'well satisfied with society as it is'

Giles in his Suffolk studio

and decrying his 'frantic adulation of the powerful, sycophancy towards the Royal Family and basic respectability.'

McInnes was well wide of the mark. Giles may well have enjoyed the company of a Royal like Prince Philip, but that did not make him a paid-up member of the Establishment. He may have made Prince Charles laugh, but he wasn't in the habit of bowing and scraping at Buckingham Palace. In any case, Colin McInnes must have forgotten about Grandma.

Grandma, as we shall see later on, allowed Giles to set up figures of the Establishment purely to knock them down again. Grandma, with her black-hat, black coat, black umbrella and (more often than not) black expression, revelled in debunking the rich and the famous and puncturing the precious egos of petty bureaucrats.

McInnes missed the crucial point. As the years rolled on, and Grandma became a national institution, she began to merge imperceptibly into Giles – and vice versa. And there was no way that

Grandma, bless her granite-coated soul, would ever have been 'well satisfied with society'. Indeed I'm surprised she didn't belt that young Mr McInnes around the head with her gnarled old umbrella handle for his impertinence.

So to understand Grandma, we must try to understand Giles – and there's no better place to begin than with a brief résumé of the cartoonist's rich and varied life.

A life in pictures

Giles was born on 29 September 1916 in Islington, north London. He was christened Ronald – and Carl came later because his haircut was startlingly reminiscent of Boris Karloff's in the film *Frankenstein*. The nickname stuck and Giles was landed with Carl as a Christian name for the rest of his life, though to his millions of fans he was always, simply, Giles.

The Giles family weren't true Londoners, although his father ran a shop in the heart of a close-knit working-class community – a far cry from the trendy, upwardly mobile New Labour Islington of today. No, their hearts were in East Anglia and it was significant that Giles made his home near Ipswich after the Second World War and

hated London with a passion for the rest of his life.

The young Giles showed an aptitude for drawing at school, but left, like so many of his contemporaries, at fourteen. He worked first as an office boy for a Wardour Street film company and then, having attracted the attention of the great film director Alexander Korda, became a cartoon animator. Working with the talented Hungarian émigré Korda was, Giles later admitted, 'the best training I could have had.'

He joined the left-wing, Co-op-owned Sunday newspaper *Reynolds News* in 1937, when he was twenty-one, and rapidly began to establish a formidable reputation as a cartoonist, specialising in single-panels and strips. His experience with Korda stood him in excellent stead, as he soon mastered composition and captured movement with the consummate ease of a seasoned professional.

When war broke out in 1939, Carl Giles was rejected for active service because of the injuries he had suffered in a motorcycle accident. Instead, he busied himself with his hugely enjoyable work at *Reynolds News* and produced a string of brilliant cartoons which portrayed war as a necessary evil, and the English soldiers as cheerful and witty as chaos reigned around them.

Inevitably, these cartoons attracted the attention of the more mainstream, national newspapers – especially the *Daily* and *Sunday Express*, whose imposing black-fronted headquarters in Fleet Street were less than a mile from *Reynolds News* in Gray's Inn Road. Lord Beaverbrook, the despotic owner of the *Express*, was determined to poach Giles – and he always got his way.

It took time, however, and John Gordon famously described the transfer as 'not an easy matter'. Eventually, after much cajoling by Gordon, the Beaverbrook shilling and the enticing prospect of a wider stage prevailed and Giles became an Express employee in the autumn of 1943. He remained one for forty-six laughter-filled, roller-coaster, turbulent years.

Inevitably, this wider stage focused Giles's vision and his mind and he began to draw a stream of classic war cartoons. Express Newspapers were so impressed that they sent their young cartoonist into the heart of the European war zone, only twelve months after they had hired him. Giles didn't mind, though. This was a chance of a lifetime.

As a war correspondent, he saw for himself the horrors of the Belsen concentration camp. Although these horrors did not lend themselves to any published Giles cartoons for more than forty-five years (he was no Goya), Giles was later to say that this horrific, heart-rending experience confirmed him as a Christian Socialist. Certainly it gave his subsequent work a gravity, humanity and both an intellectual and emotional perspective which was such an intrinsic part of his genius.

After the war, the family, dominated by the fearsome Grandma, made its first appearance. It was 5 August 1945 and the family – albeit in embryonic form – are walking along a deserted railway line with a murderous-looking Grandma bringing up the rear. They are en route for the seaside with their buckets and spades but there aren't any trains. The ironic caption reads: 'It's quicker by rail'. Giles was back from the front – with a vengeance.

It must be said that Giles's chaotic fictional family could not have been further removed from his own ordered life. In 1942 he had married his first cousin Joan 'the most beautiful woman I had ever seen' and the couple embarked upon fifty-two years of wedded bliss. They had no children. (Well, with Giles's surrogate family, there wasn't really any need, was there?)

It's quicker by rail.

Sunday Express, August 5th, 1945

For the majority of their marriage, Joan and Giles lived at an isolated farmhouse in the village of Witnesham, three miles north-east of Ipswich. Giles quickly settled into a comfortable regime, sending his cartoons to the *Daily* and *Sunday Express* by taxi and train from a penthouse studio near Ipswich station, farming his pigs, sailing on the River Deben, driving his custom-built cars (usually Bentleys) fast and drinking in the many welcoming Suffolk pubs.

By 1950, Giles was a national institution and his cartoons were an integral part of both the daily life of Britons and the tremendous success of the *Daily* and *Sunday Express*. He drew, on average, three cartoons a week – two for the daily and one for the Sunday. These were never changed by the sub-editors at Express Newspapers, who understood his value, his popularity and his bloody-mindedness! After all, he sold more papers than either the football results or the racing tips.

In 1959, Giles was awarded the OBE in recognition of his priceless ability to make the nation laugh. The Royal Family, and especially Prince Philip, who was a great fan, no doubt had their say in this honour. It was a pity, some say, that Giles was never knighted – but it would have been

A helicopter arriving to collect Giles's cartoon when he was snowbound in January 1987

ironic had such a fierce critic of the Establishment been granted one of its highest accolades.

For the next thirty years Carl Giles continued to enchant and amuse, poking fun at our ever-stranger country as it hurtled uncontrollably towards the millennium. Politicians grew more ridiculous, society became more bizarre, language more outrageous and the anarchic Giles family – steadfastly refusing to change with the times – flourished amid the mayhem.

It all had to end, of course. Giles's devoted wife, Joan, passed away on Christmas Day in 1994 and a large part of Giles died with her. Confined to a wheelchair following the amputation of both his legs in 1992, the cartoonist carried on as best he could but the will was no longer there. He died just eight months later on 27 August 1995. He was seventy-eight.

The tributes poured in from across the world. Perhaps Giles's favourite would have been from Prince Charles who wrote: 'I loved the Giles cartoons. They captured almost unerringly the mood of the nation. His gently wicked – yet never vindictive – humour endeared him to all of us in a way that no other cartoonist has achieved this century.'

This was a fitting and sensitive assessment of his work. Carl Giles would have been so proud.

A cartoonist par excellence

Giles's talent as a draughtsman and a cartoonist was so unique that it is difficult to place his work in an historical context. Nevertheless, it is worth doing so, mainly to discover his influences and to trace the visual origins of Grandma.

The most obvious predecessor of Giles is the Flemish artist Pieter Brueghel the Elder, whose vivid paintings of peasant weddings and children's games evoked the spirit of the sixteenth-century Netherlands, just as Giles evoked the spirit of Middle England in the aftermath of the Second World War and beyond. Their attention to detail, sensitivity to atmosphere and mastery of movement and perspective are uncannily similar.

Giles's lineage as a cartoonist can also be traced back to William Hogarth and Thomas Rowlandson, though he did not share Hogarth's love of moralising. But both Hogarth and Rowlandson were shrewd observers of the human condition – and so was Giles.

Giles admitted to only one influence, that of the famous Pont (Graham Laidler), whose distinctive, detailed drawings of British character were a weekly highlight of the satirical magazine *Punch* until his untimely death in 1941. Giles commented: 'When Pont died it came as the same sort of shock as when someone dies in the family. I missed his drawings and went on missing them.'

Giles also owed a debt to W. G. Baxter, the creator of the reprobate Alley Sloper, who was loved – together with his family and friends – by the Victorians in much the same way as the Giles family is loved by us today. There was, however, one major difference between these two families. The Giles family was centred on a woman, the inimitable Grandma.

Bruce Bairnsfather's Old Bill and Low's Colonel Blimp were two characters who could have walked into a Giles cartoon without anyone blinking, while the biting social observations of the great nineteenth-century French caricaturist and satirist Honoré Daumier were strikingly similar to Giles's strictures against society. Daumier was, though, rather harsher.

Giles would probably, if pushed, have acknowledged all these influences. But he was such a free-thinker and an original draughtsman that any influences were ultimately submerged beneath the weight of his own extraordinary talent. He was a one-off, whose inspiration was ultimately derived from his fertile and mischievous imagination.

Meanwhile, Carl Giles's pre-eminent place in the history of newspaper cartoons and cartoonists is assured. He simply revolutionised the art. The kind of topical and social comment he pioneered came to replace the traditional political cartoon almost everywhere and today's finest cartoonists such as Steve Bell and Posy Simmonds of the *Guardian* cite Giles as a major influence.

'He was a genius and a special hero of mine. He was also a terrific draughtsman, drawing things in detail like diesel engines that most cartoonists shrink from,' said Simmonds admiringly.

No one knew Giles's work better, nor was more qualified to speak about it, than another legendary cartoonists Sir Osbert Lancaster. Together, they were two of the very best reasons for buying the *Daily Express* in the 1960s.

Sir Osbert hit the nail on the head when he wrote: 'The work of Giles, like that of all great artists, has many aspects. There is Giles the nature-lover, Giles the recorder of intimate domestic interiors, Giles the child-lover and, of course, Giles the creator of Grandma'.

Ah yes, Grandma. This is where Grandma, clad from head-to-toe in forbidding black and wielding that fearsome umbrella, makes her dramatic entry . . .

Chapter Two

Enter Grandma – dressed in black

The earliest sighting of Grandma comes not, as one might expect, in the *Daily* or the *Sunday Express* in an ale house, a betting shop or on a street corner. No, it comes in the *Reynolds News*.

There is a cartoon dated 11 May 1941, in which a number of diminutive hooligans are clambering all

"Take no notice 'Arry. It ain't 'ers."
Reynolds News, May 11th, 1941

over a very smart Rolls Royce. The hooligan on look-out spots someone looking very like Grandma approaching and yells out: 'Take no notice, 'Arry. It ain't 'ers'. Her face isn't so grumpy and her hat isn't so squashed, but it is a proto-Grandma all right. She's dressed in black and I swear her handbag has got a padlock on it!

Peter Tory, the definitive Giles biographer, believes Grandma's first appearance occurred some seven months earlier in the *Reynolds News* on 27 October 1940.

It's the Britain of the blitz and, in true Giles style, the cartoonist is trying to cheer everyone up. So he has drawn two exasperated soldiers trying to explain to their commanding officer the trouble they are having with a little, black-coated, old lady.

'We say to her: "Friend or foe?",' complain the flummoxed solders, "and all she keeps saying is: "Foe!"'

The fact that the little old lady is smiling broadly, is carrying a white handbag and is wearing a white pinny over her coat means that she has more metamorphosing to do before she becomes the Grandma that we know and love. But Giles himself liked to say that the feisty heroine of that cartoon was the first incarnation of Grandma.

Grandma came into her own, along with the rest of the extraordinary Giles family, in the immediate aftermath of the Second World War. And what a family it was. Giles referred to them as 'the crisis family' and they certainly seemed to lurch from one chaotic incident to another. There was the work-shy father, labouring under the delusion that he was the head of the household; the harassed, dependable mother, who actually was; their bookworm son, George, who had the misfortune to be married to the snivelling hypochondriac, Vera, whose cold 'lasted from one Christmas to the next'; their small son, Ernie, prematurely bald and predisposed to dream; and the three younger ladies of the house, Ann (mother of the twins), Bridget and Carol. Oh, and we mustn't forget Butch

**"We say to her: 'Friend or Foe?'
and all she keeps saying is 'Foe!'"**
Reynolds News, October 27th, 1940

the dog or Chalkie the awful schoolmaster.

Presiding over all of these disparate, dysfunctional types was Grandma, dressed head-to-toe in black with a face like a battered pumpkin, a stomach like the Michelin man and legs like . . . well, you never saw her legs. They were permanently hidden under that tent-like coat. She was a bleakly menacing figure, drawn from the depths of Giles's subconscious, and she aroused a mixture of fear and awe in everyone who dared to cross her path.

Animals, dead rather than alive, were littered about her person. There was a bird attached to her hat, a fox slung round her neck and a bird's head doubling up as her umbrella handle. It would have been no surprise to see a black cat slink out from underneath her clothing.

By the 1950s the character – and characteristics – of Grandma were firmly lodged in the nation's psyche. She was a harridan par excellence, a source of constant amusement to the younger, more intrepid members of her family, a figure of terror to petty bureaucrats, bank managers and traffic wardens and, when she spoke, the mistress of the smart-alec, one-liner of a putdown.

Following her 'proper' debut on that deserted railway line in August 1945, Grandma soon found that the life of a Giles cartoon character could be rather fun. There she was, believe it or not, en route for the United States of America on the *Queen Mary* in the summer of 1948. She wasn't happy though – they didn't sell bull's eyes on the ship. Once back on terra firma she was glimpsed, with her back to us, bemoaning a rumoured tax on aspirins. And, yes, an embryonic Vera was by her side.

Giles, meanwhile, gave us a tantalizing glimpse of Grandma in the pen portraits of his characters in the introduction to the 1951 *Giles Annual*, the fifth in the series.

He wrote in a section headlined the *Giles Family Tree*: 'Apart from mentioning that there is always a faint sniff in the air of bull's eyes, embrocation and brandy when Grandma is around, the less said about her the better.' Well, at least we know what Grandma smells like!

Her love of racing, a constant theme during the hurly-burly of the next forty years, was the main focus of what I believe is the first definitive Grandma cartoon (16 March 1950). It's the first day of the Flat Racing Season and Grandma is out on the downs, with a telescope and a snivelling Vera by her side, when she is confronted by an irate trainer. 'Spying?', she snarls at him. 'You'd do some spying if you'd lost your old-age pension every week during the steeplechase season.'

Giles, with admirable economy, established some of Grandma's key characteristics in this one cartoon. She loves racing (echoes of the Queen Mother), she is resourceful (there's no one else on the downs that morning checking form, apart from Vera), she's profligate (the steeplechase season had proved a financial disaster) and she's proud (the uppity trainer is put firmly in his place).

"That's handy... you've left the iron on, Vera's glasses gone overboard, and grandma's sulking because they don't sell bulls'-eyes in the Queen Mary."

Daily Express, June 4th, 1948

"Keep this under your hats. I learned from a very reliable source that Cripps is going to put a hundred per cent purchase tax on aspirins."

Daily Express, April 5th, 1949

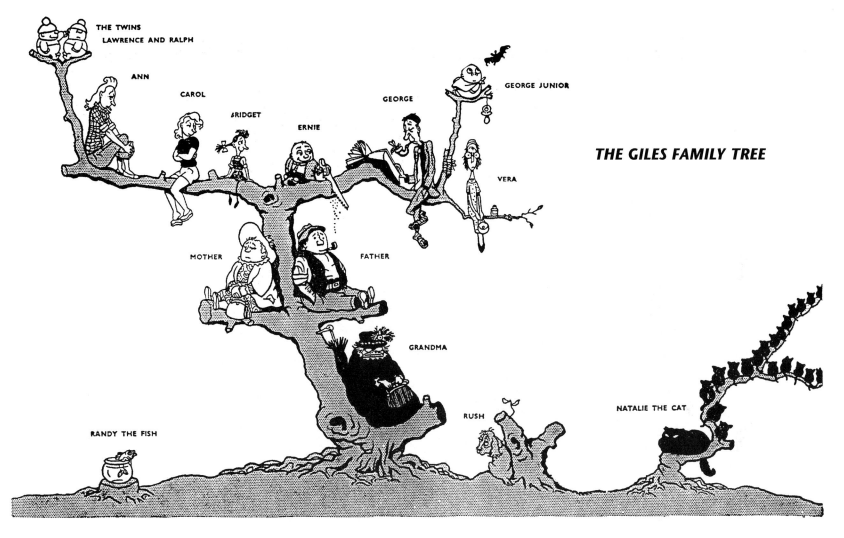

THE GILES FAMILY TREE

THE TWINS
LAWRENCE AND RALPH

ANN

CAROL

BRIDGET

ERNIE

GEORGE

GEORGE JUNIOR

VERA

MOTHER

FATHER

GRANDMA

RANDY THE FISH

RUSH

NATALIE THE CAT

He also fixed Grandma's surreal dress sense firmly in our minds, a dress sense which was always to remain steadfastly immune to the vagaries of fashion. Indeed, one wonders whether Grandma ever once changed out of her forbidding black outfit. Her hat, for example, looks as though it has been permanently clamped upon her head.

My favourite description of Grandma and her dress sense from hell comes from Peter Tory, who wrote: 'Her face was reduced to a pair of National

"Spying? You'd do some spying if you'd lost your old-age pension every week during the steeplechase season."

Daily Express, March 16th, 1950

Health specs, squeezed in between a ruffled white collar and the brim of a flat black hat, yanked on with sufficient force to keep it in place when cheering home the winner of the 4.10. The flowers on the hat got flattened and were joined by a small cloth bird. The handbag took on stouter proportions and a padlock and the armoury was completed by an umbrella of impressive proportions with a bird's head for a handle. It might be a duck, it might be a parrot, but whatever it is, its beak is quite large enough to cause actual bodily harm.'

Finally, Giles introduced a key element in Grandma's life: her relationship with Vera, the rake-thin hypochondriac. Vera is Grandma's punchbag, the butt of her jokes and the subject of her strictures. She is the Ernie Wise to Grandma's Eric Morecambe, the Stan Laurel to her Oliver Hardy. Here, Vera looks absolutely terrified by the arrival of the trainer, whilst Grandma is purely cross. Here, Vera has a tiny pair of binoculars, whilst Grandma has a massive telescope. The balance of their relationship has been firmly established.

By 1953, Grandma was beginning to attract her very own fan mail at the *Daily Express*, a sure sign that the public had taken her to their hearts. One reader, hilariously, likened her to a cactus and produced an illustration to prove it, while Grandma Moss from Manchester tried to disassociate herself from Giles's Grandma. Grandma Moss, apparently, liked bicycling, allotments and gardening, which were all outside activities loathed by Grandma. She had also once

GRANDMA G.
(REAR VIEW)

No tender plant.

Please, Giles, do not let Mrs. Moss (Express Post) persuade you to change Grandma. I am hoping to grow a small cactus, which I decided to call "Grandma" after seeing the enclosed sketch of Notocactus Leninghansii. As soon as I saw it, it reminded me of your famous old lady. (Mrs.) M. E. Kelly, Caxton Street, Derby.

won a beauty competition for her hair, but, as Giles Junior put it: 'Grandma wouldn't win a hair-do competition if she started combing right now for the next couple of hundred years.'

There are a couple of other classic Grandma cartoons from the 1950s. On 3 July 1956 Giles underlined our heroine's right-wing credentials with a cartoon of savage simplicity. Ernie and Grandma are sitting in the front row of a sparsely attended and tedious debating meeting on hanging when Ernie pipes up: 'My Grandma says hang everybody'. One look at Grandma's face – and you know she means it!

"My Grandma says hang everybody."

Daily Express, July 3rd, 1956

Incidentally, there are those who swear that Giles and Grandma were interchangeable. Here is an early indication that they were not. Grandma's political views were a million miles away from Giles's self-professed Christian socialism. Grandma would have regarded Christian socialism as a swear word, if she had known what it meant.

The other definitive cartoon was published on 8 October 1953 and once again featured Ernie as Grandma's foil. As Grandma snoozes away, Ernie's attention is caught by the newspaper headline: 'Grandmother has quads'. A visual thought bubble,

Daily Express, October 8th, 1953

25

with four baby Grandmas complete with white frizzy hair, National Health specs and black dresses, hovers dangerously over the young chap's head. He will have had nightmares for days after that.

It is usually supposed that when Grandma did venture out of the over-crowded, chaotic family home, it was to go to the pub, the betting shop, the bank or – if she fancied dipping her hand into the collection box – church. Not so. In 1958 she actually went to Ireland with the family, and tried to kiss the Blarney Stone.

This is what happened, according to a breathless Giles Junior: 'When we eventually found Grandma's feet, she put her head in the hole, and we couldn't have been holding her very tight because down she went and when we looked over the top there she was all rolled up like a big black ball, with her little boots kicking away like beetles' feet do when they roll on their backs. She must have kissed the Stone and caught the gift of the gab pretty quick, as I've never heard so many funny words in such a short space of time, including a lot of new ones.'

But Grandma wasn't finished. She was only just beginning . . .

Chapter Three

Grandma swings throughout the Sixties

The 1950s ended on a triumphant note for Giles when he was awarded the OBE in 1959. But it was in the 1960s that the Ipswich cartoonist really flourished – with Grandma to the fore.

Giles was at the height of his artistic and intellectual powers during the Swinging Sixties and he found this crazy, topsy-turvy decade to be the perfect backdrop for the equally crazy and topsy-turvy behaviour of 'the family'. Grandma may not have been out shopping in Carnaby Street every day or rolling joints and sharing a bed with Mick Jagger, but she had a damn good time nonetheless. Just look at all that booze she consumed.

When the 1960s dawned Britain was emerging from the grip of post-war austerity – and Grandma's eccentric behaviour provided welcome relief from the grey and conventional world outside. It was only a couple of years later that the rest of the country began to behave as strangely as 'the family'.

In November 1960, for example, Grandma was caught swearing violently at the television as another programme was devoted entirely to the presidential election in the United States of America. A month later, in a disturbing foretaste of the Great Train Robbery, she caused chaos amongst the mail-bags as she tried to powder her nose aboard a train. At least she said she was trying to powder her nose . . . Eat your heart out, Ronnie Biggs.

By now, Grandma was having regular run-ins

"I'm not after your mail-bags – I want to get through to powder my nose."

Sunday Express, December 4th, 1960

"Would you mind telling the old fool that everyone who calls isn't someone from the B.B.C. trying to shanghai her for 'This is Your Life'."

Daily Express, February 9th, 1961

with the authorities – or anyone who had the temerity to cross her path. In one memorable cartoon (9 February 1961) she attacked a man delivering groceries and laid out a gas board official with a solitary blow from her umbrella. Her explanation? She thought they were from the BBC, trying to get her to appear on *This Is Your Life*.

Within a couple of months she had been arrested on suspicion of being a spy (26 March 1961) for shouting 'Come on the reds' all through the Grand National and in May she was threatening Dad with a vicious-looking stick (or is it a gun?) for trying to take down a portrait of her parents from above the mantelpiece.

The aforementioned parents, or 'folks' as Grandma calls them, are a gruesome duo. Father is a moustachioed military type, who looks as though he'd bolt at the first sound of gunfire, while mother is clearly the harridan from hell. (Mind you, she'd have to be pretty tough, to give birth to Grandma!)

In fact, it transpires that mother didn't just give birth to Grandma. At the risk of stretching the imagination to the very limit, it has to be pointed out that Grandma had at least three other siblings, including two sisters 'from the north'. Dressed in identical black coats and hats, with foxes slung around their shoulders, they turned up in Blackpool in December 1963.

The consequences of having Grandma in the household were pretty dire, but the family bore her presence with remarkable fortitude. There were times when patience wore thin, notably when her magnificent tummy rumble sounded more like an earthquake or a fifty-megatoner (31 October 1961) or when she took to smoking a vile-smelling pipe in a vain attempt to give up cigarettes (11 March 1962).

But Grandma was a law unto herself and always would be – as pompous bureaucrats, traffic wardens, travelling salesmen, policemen, church wardens, politicians, bank managers and other examples of petty officialdom found increasingly to their cost.

She began 1962 by bedding down in a splendid £15,000 yacht at the International Boat Show (it was a cold, cold winter), before being surprised by an outraged official who yelled: 'We don't think Madam is remotely interested in purchasing a yacht – we think Madam has just looked in to thaw her tootsies.' A rare sighting of Grandma's stockinged feet, poking out from underneath her coat, confirmed this diagnosis.

"Of course we know you're not a spy, Grandma. On the other hand, if you hadn't kept hollering 'Come on the Reds' all through the Grand National..."

Sunday Express, March 26th, 1961

"You heard what Salisbury said about the Lords – 'It should not be open to everyone to repudiate the responsibilities their ancestors imposed on them.' That picture of my folks stays."

Daily Express, May 9th, 1961

"That wasn't a fifty-megatoner or an earthquake – that was Grandma's tummy rumbling."

Daily Express, October 31st, 1961

"Grandma, forty cigarettes a day for the last sixty-odd years haven't done you any harm — why change now?."

Sunday Express, March 11th, 1962

"We don't think Madam is remotely interested in purchasing a £15,000 yacht – we think Madam has just looked in to thaw her tootsies."

Daily Express, January 2nd, 1962

"Grandma, if you can't take your ice skates off stop stamping your feet to get warm."

Sunday Express, January 27th, 1963

Grandma's feet were still giving her problems a year later. Admittedly it was the worst winter in living memory, but did she really have to wear her ice skates to church and stamp her feet noisily to keep warm (27 January 1963)?

In the 1950s Grandma hadn't been too interested in politicians who were, by and large, fairly remote and patrician figures. By the 1960s, however, politicians were becoming increasingly over-familiar with the public (and, in the case of War Minister John Profumo, with Christine Keeler) and they were upsetting Grandma with their airs and graces and the promises they never had any intention of keeping.

So it comes as no surprise to see Grandma setting off to the Conservative Party Conference in Llandudno (9 October 1962) armed with a wonderful collection of rotting cabbages, eggs and tomatoes – ready to do battle with what turned out to be the fag-end of Harold Macmillan's government. In a delightfully unobtrusive Giles touch, a snooty Tory grandee looks down his elongated nose at Grandma, blissfully unaware that the cabbages could soon be heading straight for him.

Clearly, the rotten cabbages did not have the desired effect because Grandma was still on the political warpath on Budget Day (2 April) the following year, threatening her terrified local postmaster with the words: 'If it's all off income tax and nothing on pensions don't be around on Budget Thursday morning, my lad'.

This brings us to the trick question of Grandma and money. She rarely had any. When she starts to study form for the 1963 Derby, the cry in the household goes up: 'Watch your piggy banks.'

Church, meanwhile, was proving to be a happy hunting ground for Grandma. Apart from warming her feet at morning service by banging her skates up and down, she also found time to get rid of her last 'green stamps' in the collection (8 December 1963). Although she attended church regularly, it would not be totally accurate to say that Grandma was God-fearing. It is more likely that God was Grandma-fearing.

Church may or may not have given Grandma spiritual sustenance, but whisky certainly did. In the week (19 January 1964) that the price of whisky was slashed from 41 shillings and six pence (that's £2.08 pence, rounded up) to just 35 shillings (£1.75 pence), Grandma loaded her supermarket trolley with five bottles of Scotch – and nothing else. A

"One return, Llandudno."

Daily Express, October 9th, 1962

"If it's all off income tax and nothing on pensions don't be around on Thursday morning, my lad."

Daily Express, April 2nd, 1963

"When Grandma starts studying form watch your piggy-banks, I always say."

Daily Express, May 28th, 1963

"There go the last of grandma's green stamps."

Sunday Express, December 8th, 1963

"They're not going to like it at home – spending the week's grocery money on Scotch."

Sunday Express, January 19th, 1964

"Excuse me while I have a word with this Mod about transistor radios."

Sunday Express, May 17th, 1964

"I've run her round the shops, called on her sister Ivy, dropped her off for an hour's bingo – and I still bet the old faggot votes the other way."

Daily Express, October 15th, 1964

terrified Vera sounded a warning note, saying: 'They're not going to like it at home – spending the week's grocery money on Scotch.' Did that worry Grandma? Certainly not.

By the summer of 1964, the Mods were in full swing, and so was Grandma. There she was, interrupting the idyll of a village cricket match by playing her transistor radio at full blast. Not even the baying of several retired colonels, who looked as though they had escaped from the Long Room at Lords, could shut Grandma – or her radio – up.

The General Election of October 1964 saw Grandma very much in demand – by the politicians. One cartoon saw Grandma being dropped off at the polling station by a motley crew of party hangers-on, together with the candidate and the agent, who says in a disgruntled voice: 'I've run her round the shops, called on her sister Ivy, dropped her off for an hour's bingo – and I still bet the old faggot votes the other way.'

That's one of the reasons why we love Grandma; she plays the politicians at their own game. (By the way, I doubt very much whether Grandma would have been to see her sister Ivy, who lives in the north of England or, possibly, Scotland. But that's a minor quibble.) Of more significance is the description of Grandma as 'an old faggot.' Clearly, the meaning of this particular insult has changed over the years. Today, I am sure that anyone who dared to address the formidable lady thus would receive a sound thrashing with her umbrella.

The question of Grandma's geographical antecedents, raised by the reference to her sister Ivy, was partially answered a couple of years later

"You don't need an interpreter to translate Grandma's comments. Her wee Grandpa came from bonnie Dundee."

Daily Express, November 8th, 1966

when Grandma was pictured holding a paper with the headline 'Girl sacked for her Scots accent' and shouting and swearing for all she was worth. Of course, it could be that she was confusing Scots with Scotch, but the more likely explanation for her fury is that her own Grandpa came from Dundee.

Grandma was also a great cynic. At the height of the *I'm Backing Britain* campaign, which took the country by storm at the beginning of 1968, she had great pleasure in pointing out that gullible Vera's Buy-British, Union Jack-emblazoned carrier bag actually had *Made In Tokyo* written on the bottom in small print. Giles obviously believed that this rather silly outbreak of phoney patriotism needed ridiculing, and Grandma was the perfect person to do it.

This wasn't the first time that Grandma acted as the cartoonist's mouthpiece. But that does not mean, as we shall see later on during this book, that Grandma was Giles.

As 1968 progressed, Grandma's mood became increasingly upbeat, combative and confrontational. She had no intention of subscribing to the concepts of peace, love and understanding which were the cornerstones of the burgeoning hippie movement. She contented herself with throwing

Labour minister Barbara Castle over her shoulder (30 April), screaming at the Post Office for increasing the price of stamps (15 September) and stealing from the church collection (22 September).

Hell hath no fury like Grandma on the rampage. But she still managed to enjoy a robust belly-laugh when she suggested to a terrified Vera that the doctor might 'have your heart out and shove it in Mrs Harris before you can say Happy New Year'. Grandma certainly found the possibilities of Dr Christian Barnard's ground-breaking heart surgery fascinating.

By the end of the year she was ransacking the children's piggy banks again, but Ernie was one step ahead of her. With a knowing smile, he explained: 'She'll be lucky. Because of the grave international monetary crisis I took the precaution of removing the contents of me piggy bank this time.'

Whilst Grandma may have presented a formidable persona to the outside world, she was occasionally a trifle insecure inside. She was aware that she wasn't immortal and, with the rise of the private residential and nursing homes in the 1970s and 1980s, she could have been removed permanently from the family home. Now and

"Down there in the small print, Vera me girl – 'MADE IN TOKYO'."

Sunday Express, January 14th, 1968

"It's the old fool who said she'd report us to Barbara Castle for putting a penny on her embrocation."

Daily Express, April 30th, 1968

"As the Bank Rate's been cut ½% may I suggest that this week you put something in instead of whipping something out."

Sunday Express, September 22nd, 1968

"Watch 'im Vera – he'll have your heart out and shove it in Mrs Harris before you can say Happy New Year."

Daily Express, January 4th, 1968

"Put the doctor down, Grandma. He's come about Ernie's measles, not to bump you off."

Daily Express,
May 2nd, 1969

51

"The young man says they're called purple hearts with LSD – they taste ever so nice."

Sunday Express, August 31st, 1969

"What's so special about Grandma's feet that she mustn't get oil on them like everybody else? ."

Daily Express, May 27th, 1969

again this insecurity rose to the surface, such as when she grabbed the doctor around the neck and wrestled him to the ground. He had only come about Ernie's measles, but Grandma had read the headlines in the paper advocating euthanasia for those over eighty. She wasn't taking any chances.

There were times, too, when Giles thought about bumping her off. But Grandma's creator realised that the spiritual and physical void her death would leave would be immense. So she remained, a sprightly 'Eightysomething', forever – comfortably outliving Giles himself.

She could have died at the Isle of Wight pop festival in 1969, which featured Bob Dylan and The Who, where she and Vera took a potentially lethal mixture of purple hearts and LSD . . . but survived to tell the tale. Quite what Grandma and Vera were doing in the middle of a load of spaced-out hippies was never explained, but – as a rule – it is best not to seek a rational explanation for their behaviour.

In May 1969 we were treated to a rare and tantalizing glimpse of Grandma's feet, presumably none the worse for her mind-bending experiences on the Isle of Wight. The *Torrey Canyon* disaster, in which an oil tanker went aground, caused widespread pollution on Britain's beaches. But Grandma, of course, was unperturbed and she engaged Ernie and the twins to carry her around in a deckchair, feet exposed, as the oil lapped below.

This was a vintage year for Grandma. She was busy punching hell out of a fellow member of her church congregation in an attempt to be 'Church Militant' (24 August); dumping her rubbish in a forest, with a policeman in vain pursuit, during the dustmen's strike (12 October); causing havoc in a hunt because the hounds thought she was concealing a fox under that voluminous coat; and burping loudly throughout the Christmas service (23 December).

And on 30 December 1969, Grandma fans received a real treat as the innermost secrets of her bedroom were revealed. This was – and is – a genuine 'Through The Keyhole' experience.

The cartoon was, I suspect, simply a device to open up an Aladdin's cave of Grandma goodies. The younger members of the family had hijacked her room in order to put their Christmas present, a scrawny-looking kitten, to bed because it had flu. Grandma appeared on the scene like an avenging angel and it would be pretty safe to assume that the kitten would have been removed in double-quick time.

"When I said I'd like to see more evidence of the 'Church Militant' in our little flock I did not mean having three rounds with Mrs Wilkins after morning service."

Sunday Express, August 24th, 1969

"With a bit of luck we'll lose him in this fog then WOOSH! away it goes."

Sunday Express, October 12th, 1969

"Madam, my dogs insist that you are concealing at least one fox under there."

Sunday Express, November 2nd, 1969

"My Grandma swallowed three holly berries in her cornflakes this morning."

Sunday Express, December 23rd, 1969

"Don't fly off the handle, Grandma – we're only using your bed while our Christmas present's got flu."
Daily Express,
December 30th, 1969

59

"Mum, are you sure Grandma's the right one to be carrying on their lessons while the teachers are on strike?"

Daily Express, February 19th, 1970

So what's in the room? The eye is immediately caught by a series of pictures which give a number of fascinating clues about Grandma's family and her past. Above her bed hangs Albert, who bears an uncanny resemblance to Buster Merryweather's grandfather character in *Only Fools And Horses* and is a convict from Botany Bay. (I suspect that the roguish Albert is Grandma's grandpa.)

We have already stumbled across Grandma's parents, her insipid-looking moustachioed father and her battle-axe of a mother, and there they are – hanging on either side of her bed. Cousin Morris, a jockey, hangs there too. And Morris knows a lot about hanging – he was hanged in 1902!

Grandma's bedside table is revolting. Cigarette ends, spilling out of the ashtray, are strewn everywhere. A jar of horse oil jostles for pride of place with a bottle of brown ale, while a box of matches lies dangerously near the bedside lamp. The overall smell, one imagines, would have been pretty pungent.

As the 1970s dawned, so did the strikes. Grandma's approach to the infuriating disruption these caused was both pragmatic and entrepreneurial. Whilst Giles, as a socialist, might have had some sympathy with the dockers, the

"I hope not. Oh boy, I hope not."

Sunday Express, April 5th, 1970

"If any four-year-old in this family won £25,000 I know into whose greedy little hands it would pass."

Sunday Express, May 17th, 1970

"I think you're as safe kissing Butch as you know who."

Daily Express,
September 17th, 1970

postmen, the dustmen and the teachers, Grandma did not. We have already seen her dump rubbish in a forest during the dustmen's strike, and she was soon teaching rubbish during the teachers' strike (19 February 1970), using a succession of (sometimes) misspelled racing terms to explain the alphabet.

Young Ernie, meanwhile, was still dreaming those weird and wonderful dreams (5 April 1970). On spotting a newspaper headline asserting that an obsession with nudity was spreading across the country, he took one look at a fully clothed Grandma and Vera and shuddered: 'I hope not. Oh boy, I hope not.'

Ernie was clearly none too enamoured with Grandma in 1970. When he read that a four-year-old had won £25,000 worth of premium bonds (17 May), he muttered: 'If any four-year-old in this family won £25,000 I know into whose greedy little hands it would soon pass'. Grandma, meanwhile, is seen slinking into The Red Lion public house.

Another newspaper headline, which suggested that it was dangerous to kiss pets, set Ernie off again (19 September). He took one look at Grandma and announced, to no one in particular, that: 'It's as safe to kiss Butch the dog as you know who.' As Grandma had passed out from a surfeit of booze and fags, he was probably right.

Ernie was clearly enjoying his role as chief commentator on Grandma's many foibles and excesses. As Grandma worked up a head of indignant steam during the postal strike in the spring of 1971 and fired off a succession of letters (which could not, of course, be posted), Ernie reflected wryly: 'Boy! I'm glad I'm not editor of the *Dear Sir* column when the post strike ends.'

A gentle canter through all of Giles's cartoons over the years might not have made it clear whether it was mum or dad who was Grandma's child. All is revealed, though, on 21 March 1971 when dad gives Grandma some flowers on Mothering Sunday. Grandma, of course, would have preferred a bottle of Scotch – and says so.

She got her own back on Father's Day that year, however, by drinking dad's present of a bottle of whisky and passing out. Possibly in retaliation, the whole family ignored a spurious-sounding anniversary called Grandma Day on 10 October, despite the fact that Grandma had covered the whole house in posters announcing the event.

Throughout the 1970s Grandma continued to hit the nail – and a number of other assorted people

"Boy! I'm glad I'm not editor editor of the 'Dear Sir' column when the post strike ends."

Daily Express, March 4th, 1971

"Damn flowers – never a bottle of Scotch."

Sunday Express, March 21st, 1971

"Who's been having a go at the bottle of whisky we bought Dad for Father's Day?"

Sunday Express, June 20th, 1971

"Know what we forgot?"

Sunday Express, October 10th, 1971

"Off transistors! Nothing puts Grandma in her let's-hang-everybody mood quicker than Wonderful Radio One."

Daily Express, October 17th, 1971

"*Grandma says she's on the side of the miners yet she belts me one every time the lights go off.*"

Daily Express, February 15th, 1972

"That's Grandma's fuel saving for the day – good night party political broadcasts."

Daily Express,
January 24th, 1974

"FOURTEEN PLEASE!"

Daily Express, December 5th, 1974

and objects – firmly on the head. She railed against the trivial self-trumpeting of the truly awful *'Wonderful Radio One'* (17 October 1971); supported the miners but hated it when the lights went off (15 February 1972); smashed the television during a party political broadcast (24 January 1974); asked for 15 loaves during the baker's strike (5 December 1974); swore profusely to celebrate the arrival of punk rock (5 December 1976); and belted out a 41-gun salute to celebrate the birth of Princess Anne's first child (16 November 1977).

Meanwhile, as the 1970s progressed, we learned a little more about Grandma's past – or did we? It's over to Ernie again. 'According to Grandma,' he

"THAT one is high in the 4-letter charts if you could hear her."

Sunday Express, December 5th, 1976

"Grandma! Major Jones doesn't like your forty-one gun salute."

(To H.R.H. Princess Anne and Capt. Mark Phillips A Son)

Daily Express, November 16th, 1977

"According to Grandma, she worked hard all her life; brought up 14 children on 10 shillings a week; did 12 hours a day down a mine; got a Karate Black Belt; and she's very happy."

Daily Express, September 23rd, 1977

"I wouldn't be Bobby Robson if they lose, and I wouldn't be the Arsenal team if __they__ win."

Daily Express, May 5th, 1978

"We know your team won. Never mind how he got it – take it back!"

said somewhat sceptically in the autumn of 1977, 'she worked hard all her life; brought up 14 children on 10 shillings a week; did 12 hours a day down a mine; got a Karate Black Belt; and she's very happy.'

Ernie was reflecting on a newspaper headline that would have given women's libbers like Germaine Greer apoplexy. It read: 'Women should work harder, die earlier and be happier.' (Sounds like it could have been written by Alf Garnett, the wonderful brainchild of Johnny Speight, one of Giles's dearest friends.)

While we needn't believe everything Grandma says about her past (or, indeed, anything), we can be certain that she (like Giles) was an Ipswich Town supporter – even though she originally came from Scotland. This was emphatically and triumphantly confirmed when Ipswich won the FA Cup Final in 1978, beating Arsenal 1–0.

On the eve of the Cup Final (5 May), a rosette-bedecked Grandma was in a wild frame of mind, swinging a vicious-looking cat-o'-nine-tails above her head and threatening all manner of retribution to everyone if Ipswich lost. Luckily for everyone concerned, they didn't.

Readers of the *Daily Express* may have wondered how Grandma celebrated this historic win, because Giles did not reveal anything in the paper. Instead, he drew a special cartoon for the Ipswich Town Football Club directors, which still has pride of place at the club. This cartoon, which shows a delirious rattle-wielding Grandma returning home with Butch and the FA Cup, is published here for the first time.

Consequently, as the 1970s climaxed with the election of Margaret Thatcher as Prime Minister, Grandma was in boisterous spirits. And so she should have been. For at last there was someone running the country who bore – in views and character, if not in looks – more than a passing resemblance to herself.

That was Giles's genius. He had anticipated the arrival of Mrs Thatcher, a no-nonsense, plain-talking, handbag-swinging matriarch who spoke directly to the heart of Middle England. And he – and Grandma – were ready and waiting.

Chapter Four

The decade of the matriarch

It is highly unlikely that Grandma toasted Margaret Thatcher's victory at the 1979 General Election with anything more than a brown ale, a cigarette and a trip to the bookmakers. She was always deeply suspicious of politicians – and Mrs Thatcher would have been no exception.

Yet Thatcher's radical redrawing of the political landscape, her ability to speak in a voice which Middle England understood (until she lost it with the Poll Tax) and the fact that she was a woman and, in 1989, a grandmother, made her an ideal vehicle for Carl Giles and the perfect foil for Grandma.

Clearly the election had put Grandma in a good mood because, within a couple of weeks of Thatcher's arrival at Downing Street, she was cracking one of her rare jokes (7 June 1979). The scene was the doctor's surgery, a favourite venue for Grand-ma's sporadic wisecracks, and she wore a huge grin as she said: 'Nothing serious, Doc – that large bump on your right side is only your wallet.' Doctors, you see, had just been given a massive pay rise.

By April 1980 Grandma was in distinct Thatcher-ite mode. As she left a soothing performance of *The Desert Song* by the Arcadian Amateur Dramatic Society, she complained: 'Not bad – could do with a few beheadings and floggings to liven it up.' Luckily for Grandma, the Falklands War was only a couple of years away.

In the summer of the same year another famous grandmother was in the news. It was the Queen Mother's eightieth birthday and Grandma was celebrating with a large Guinness for breakfast. Ernie remonstrated, arguing that the Queen Mum was rather more temperate.

Meanwhile JR and *Dallas* fever was sweeping

"Nothing serious, Doc – that large bump on your right side is only your wallet."

Daily Express, June 7th, 1979

"Not bad – could do with a few beheadings and floggings to liven it up."

Daily Express, April 13th, 1980

"I'll bet the Royal Grandma doesn't start her birthday celebrations
with a large Guinness for breakfast."

Daily Express, July 15th, 1980

Britain, fuelled by the then ubiquitous disc jockey and television presenter, Terry Wogan. Grandma caught the mood of the country perfectly when she placed £5 on Wogan in the *Dallas Whodunnit Stakes*, arguing: 'If he isn't on the *Dallas* show, it's the only one he ain't' (27 May 1980). Later (23 November 1980), she refused to pay out on Kristin shooting JR – because she had dozed off when it was revealed 'who dunnit'!

That Christmas, Grandma was in heaven with the release of a truly awful record called *There's No One Quite Like Grandma*. She listened to the record, which reached number two in the charts, ninety-three times in a record shop without buying it (18 December).

Grandma's patriotism, one of her most marked and constant traits, came to the fore with the 'fairytale wedding' of Prince Charles and Lady Diana Spencer in the summer of 1981. She painted her traditional black coat, hat and padlocked handbag the colours of the Union Jack, terrifying Butch the dog in the process, and set off to Westminster Abbey rather than St Paul's Cathedral because 'they always have 'em there.'

And, before Grandma's patriotic fervour had had time to die down, there came the Falklands War. Giles's simple cartoon, which showed Grandma dancing in the streets, waving a Union Jack and ringing a bell, said it all. This wasn't a universal reaction to the outbreak of war, but the victory which ensued won the next General Election for the decade's other great matriarch.

It wasn't long before Grandma was clearing out her old air-raid shelter with tremendous gusto (4 April 1982) then celebrating at the height of the war, when it was clear that we were winning, by taking to a choppy river with Vera, Ernie, Butch et al in the most rickety of boats. A wary boatman shouted after her. 'Off you go and rejoice – and steer clear of the Falklands 200-mile restricted zone' (2 May 1982).

Luckily, Grandma did not end up in the Falklands 200-mile restricted zone, where she would have undoubtedly caused a major diplomatic incident, and she was back a week or so later on terra firma, berating an affluent-looking Home Counties couple for flying the Union Jack upside down.

She was also back in the doctor's surgery, scene of some of her finest hours, where she warned a terrified Vera that their GP might hypnotise her for 'sex romps' (25 November 1982). Poor Vera, she wouldn't have known what a sex romp was if she'd

"Fiver Terry Wogan, because if he isn't on the Dallas show it's the only one he ain't."

Daily Express, May 27th, 1980

stumbled right into the middle of one. And the doctor didn't look too happy at Grandma's suggestion, either!

As the 1980s progressed, Grandma appeared to become more and more of a political animal. Rumours, spread by Ernie, that she might have written the *Hitler Diaries* (26 April 1983) proved unfounded, but that didn't prevent her taking a

"She won't pay out on this Kristin shooting JR – she says she dozed off when they showed who dunnit."

Sunday Express, November 23rd, 1980

"Lady, you've played it 93 times – are you going to buy the bloody thing or not?"

Daily Express, December 18th, 1980

"You'll have to take it off Grandma – Butch doesn't like it."

Sunday Express, July 26th, 1981

"I told her it's at St. Paul's but she says they always have 'em here."

Daily Express, July 29th, 1981

"But when the blast of war blows in our ears ... Stiffen the sinews, Summon up the blood ... Clear out the old air-raid shelter ...."

Sunday Express, April 4th, 1982

"Off you go and rejoice – and steer clear of the Falklands 200 mile restricted zone."

Daily Express, May 2nd, 1982

"Psst! It's upside down."

Daily Express, May 11th, 1982

keen interest in the events of the day – and giving a startled and indignant Mrs Thatcher a piece of her mind (30 December 1986).

This new-found interest in the political scene fascinated Ernie, the Grandma-watcher par excellence. 'Grandma on politics,' he mused. 'She'd give Hurricane Higgins fourteen rounds in the ring with Frank Bruno and then send them up to Liverpool to give Derek Hatton a hammering.' (3 October 1985). Grandma, meanwhile, was busy doing something very odd in the dustbin.

Her political preoccupations were driving the family mad. She was even promised a knighthood, allegedly by Downing Street, if she laid off politics for five minutes so her long-suffering relatives could have a nap (8 February 1986). They should be so lucky – silence is an alien concept to Grandma, unless she's passed out.

She had also taken to betting on the most unlikely scenarios, i.e. Terry Wogan for Prime Minister and Michael Heseltine for *EastEnders* (14 January 1986), a double which presumably kept the bookmakers in champagne for a couple of weeks – and Grandma in purdah.

She was out on Britain's mean streets again by May that year, though, when a few well-directed swishes of her umbrella put a couple of yobs to flight. Surveying her handiwork, she commented: 'If I were Mrs Thatcher and had to choose between cleaning up the Middle East or cleaning up dirty Britain, I'd choose the Middle East.'

She was certainly more than a match for a neo-Nazi punk rocker who tried to steal her pension book. The punk quailed as Grandma raised her fist to strike him (15 November 1987) and it would be safe to assume that this unnerving experience was enough to put him off attacking old ladies for good.

Meanwhile, Grandma was an enthusiastic part of the Thatcher share revolution, applying for 10,000 British Telecom shares but receiving none (4 December 1984) and leaving her gas fire on all day so she could make a profit on her British Gas shares (25 November 1986). That second stunt comes straight out of the *Alice In Wonderland* book of logic.

Then, in September 1988, Grandma received a personal request from Mrs Thatcher that would have made her fox fur quiver with pride. The Prime Minister had just heard that she was about to become a grandmother and wondered whether Grandma – the queen of all grannies – would like a

"Watch 'im Vera."

Daily Express, November 25th, 1982

"*I didn't SAY she wrote them – I only said she COULD have written them.*"

Daily Express, April 26th, 1983

"Thank you so much for calling and advising me on the changes I must make in 1987. Now hop it."

Daily Express, December 30th, 1986

"Grandma on politics... she'd give Hurricane Higgins 14 rounds in the ring with Frank Bruno,
then send them both up to Liverpool to give Derek Hatton a hammering."

Daily Express, October 3rd, 1985

"10 Downing Street say they will give Grandma a knighthood if she will lay off politics for five minutes so we can have a nap."

Daily Express, February 9th, 1986

"What odds will we give her on Wogan to move into No. 10 and Heseltine to take over Dirty Den on TV?"

Daily Express, January 14th, 1986

"If I was Mrs Thatcher and had to choose between cleaning up the MIddle East or cleaning up dirty Britain I'd choose the Middle East."

Daily Express, May 29th, 1986

"Watch it! I can get you 2½ years inside if you hit me just because I nicked your pension book."

Sunday Express, November 15th, 1987

"Whoa there! We warned you if you went for over 100,000 Telecom shares you might end up with none!"

Daily Express, December 4th, 1984

Downing Street job as an Advisory Executive. For some reason Grandma never took up this post – perhaps she was worried that the Downing Street atmosphere might have been, shall we say, a trifle claustrophobic.

By the time that Mrs Thatcher had uttered the immortal words 'We are a Grandmother', Grandma was in a pretty foul mood, prompting Ernie to complain (5 March 1989): 'We are a Grandmother, but I don't think we are amused'. The reason, I suspect, for Grandma's non-amusement was the sudden appearance of a cactus on her windowsill which bore an uncanny resemblance to her. (Prickly – or what?)

Grandma soon cheered up, however, when she learned that call girls were working at the House of Commons (16 March 1989). So she popped along to Westminster to see if she might offer MPs a little bit on the side – just light cleaning and tea-making, of course. Surprisingly, given the sexual proclivities of some MPs, no one took Grandma up on her generous proposition.

Undaunted, she then applied for the Prime Minister's job itself when Mrs Thatcher found herself the victim of a very Conservative coup in the late autumn of 1990. Unfortunately, as a policeman told her on the steps of 10 Downing Street, the job was for MPs only.

She was still on the political trail a couple of weeks later – when Alf Garnett was cast adrift by the BBC in much the same back-stabbing manner in which Mrs Thatcher was knifed by the Conservatives. Grandma had the solution (18 November) and stormed over to her MP's house to press her hero's claims for Number 10. Now, Alf would have been an interesting choice.

Anyway John Major, a safer bet than Alf, got Mrs Thatcher's job and his appointment ushered in a grey political regime in which there was no place for outspoken, chain-smoking, hard-drinking, umbrella-wielding, right-wing grandmothers. Grandma's political work was done.

She bowed out gracefully, allowing Butch to slip his lead and go to Paris for lunch via the embryonic Channel Tunnel (4 November), before heading for the snug in her local pub, putting her feet up and downing a swift Scotch or three.

Well, she had come a long way since those distant, sepia-tinted days of nearly half a century ago – and she certainly deserved a rest.

"I'm trying to work out her arithmetic – she buys a half dozen British Gas shares then leaves her gasfire on all day so they make a profit."

Daily Express, November 25th, 1986

"The lady says she's going to be a grandma and would you like a Downing Street job as an Advisory Executive?"

Sunday Express, September 4th, 1988

"'We are a Grandmother', but I don't think 'we' are amused."

Sunday Express, March 5th, 1989

*"I'd like to take advantage of earning a bit on the side – just light cleaning
and tea-making, of course."*

Daily Express, March 16th, 1989

"She's not in a very good mood – we've been knocking on 10 Downing Street all afternoon and the Policeman told her the job's for MPs only."

Daily Express, 1990

"Please tell my MP I've got another candidate for him to vote for."

Sunday Express, November 18th, 1990

"Butch has slipped his lead and gone off to Paris for lunch."

Sunday Express, November 4th, 1990

Chapter Five

The $64,000 question:
So who was Grandma?

The hunt to discover the model for Grandma would have baffled detectives as famous and intelligent as Sherlock Holmes and Hercule Poirot. The Grandma trail is so full of cul-de-sacs, false leads and red herrings, mostly orchestrated and planted by Giles himself, that it can be confusing trying to make sense of all the clues.

Every friend, colleague and admirer of Giles has a theory about Grandma's origins. And each theory is different – although most people agree that there was an element of Giles himself in his wonderful creation, especially as he grew older, more intolerant and more irascible.

The most sensible place to start in this labyrinthine journey, is with Giles's own grandmothers. Neither, it must be said at the outset, had much in common with Grandma, but their dual presence must have lodged in his subconscious as a child for him to devise such a powerful, larger-than-life character.

Giles said that there was a bit of both his grandmothers in Grandma, but it is extremely difficult to pinpoint which bits. Neither had a raging thirst (for alcohol), a padlocked handbag or a penchant for stealing from the church collection. Both were well-balanced, kindly souls whose view of the world was more tranquil than their fictional counterpart.

His father's mother was a handsome Victorian lady who commanded both affection and respect (no similarities there, then). Her husband was a jockey who rode for Edward VII, which Grandma would have loved, and she was confined to a wheelchair in her later years, which Grandma would have hated. She didn't drink, apart from the occasional medicinal brandy.

His mother's mother was even softer and kinder. Nanny Clarke, as she was known, lived in Norwich and the young Giles loved to get away from the hustle and bustle of London to visit her. She was instrumental, therefore, in instilling a lifelong love of East Anglia into Giles. She liked a social drink, unlike Grandma who liked an anti-social drink, and presided over a happy and friendly household. (No connection there, then.)

So where did Grandma come from? Ultimately, she sprang from Giles's extremely fertile imagination and, consequently, carried a part of her creator around with her. It began as a small part but, like Topsy, just grew and grew and grew.

Giles's great friend and drinking companion, Johnny Speight, the creator of television's Alf Garnett (who would have made Grandma an interesting husband), once said: 'I have no doubt at all that Giles is there in Grandma all the way through. She has his spirit and his mischief. She is the scourge of everything which Giles hates, after all – everything from VAT inspectors to traffic wardens get walloped. Of course, he's Grandma.'

Up to a point. It is certainly true that Giles and Grandma shared a number of characteristics and habits, and Giles hinted – and once or twice said outright – that he was Grandma, but there are two crucial differences. Well, three actually, if you count the fact that Giles was a man and Grandma was a woman.

First, Grandma was often the butt of everyone else's jokes and Giles, a proud and sensitive man, would have never tolerated that. There was no way that he would have allowed the rest of his family to dance around his chair (or wheelchair in later years) and make fun of him. He wouldn't have appreciated the joke.

Secondly, their politics were very different. Giles referred to himself as a Christian Socialist and Grandma was deeply suspicious of both Christians and Socialists. The combination of the two would have sent her scurrying for her smelling salts and her Scotch.

Nevertheless, the myth that Giles and Grandma were one and the same evolved slowly into fact, often fostered by Giles himself. They did look similar, especially in a couple of self-portraits that he did for friends. In one, given to the landlord and landlady of his beloved Maybush public house at Waldringfield, near Woodbridge in Suffolk, Giles is staring into a shaving mirror and Grandma, eerily, is staring back at him.

And when questioned closely by Yvonne Ward, the manageress of the bar at the Centrespot restaurant at Ipswich Town Football Club, Giles said emphatically: 'I am Grandma.' There was though, says Yvonne, a twinkle in his eye when he imparted this crucial piece of information to her.

The problem is, as Yvonne admitted, that it was always incredibly difficult to tell when Giles was telling the truth and when he was spinning a line. He probably didn't know himself half the time, especially after a few glasses of whisky. (Now whisky is something that he had in common with Grandma!)

Whisky was probably flowing on another occasion when Giles remarked to a close friend: 'I'm like Grandma's brother, only worse.' For once, Giles might have been being a little harsh on himself.

Meanwhile, if Giles did look like Grandma, he wasn't the only one. For example Valerie Maddison, who lives in Ipswich, believes that her grandmother, Emily, was the spitting image of Grandma. And she is prepared to go one step further – she is convinced that Giles modelled Grandma on Emily.

Before Valerie's claims are dismissed out of hand as delusions of grandeur, it should be pointed out that Giles and Valerie's father, Frank, were great drinking companions and spent many a happy hour in the welcoming environment of Suffolk's pubs.

They met after the Second World War, when Giles upped sticks from London and moved to Witnesham, and Frank was on leave from the RAF. On some of these occasions, Frank's mother, Emily, would come along for the ride and she and Giles got to know each other quite well.

'The physical resemblance between my gran and Grandma was utterly uncanny. They were both quite small in height, but very round. They both wore hats with some kind of bird stuck on them, they both had long black shapeless coats which touched the ground and they both had spectacles which looked as though they were wedged permanently on to their faces,' recalled Valerie.

'As far as I was concerned, gran was Grandma, if you see what I mean,' smiled Valerie. 'Dad always thought so and Giles never denied it. He had every

Was this Grandma? Mrs Emily Andrews pictured (back, far right) with her family just after the Second World War

chance to deny it if he wanted to, but he never did,' she explained.

'He was a lovely man and I knew he was exceptionally fond of our family. I think it would have been his way of paying a small tribute to us by using my gran as a model for Grandma. But he would never have let on – that wasn't his style,' Valerie added.

One small but crucial point, of which Valerie was probably unaware, gives credence to her claims. Grandma began to evolve as a fully fledged Giles cartoon character from 1945 onwards, precisely from the time that Giles and Valerie's father began to drink together. She blossomed as their friendship blossomed.

And, interestingly enough, when that friendship petered out as Valerie's father spent more and more time abroad with the RAF, Giles rekindled his links with the family by drinking regularly with Valerie a decade or so later. I wonder whether Giles felt a special affinity with Frank and Valerie's family because of Grandma.

It would be wrong, though, to suggest that Valerie's granny, or Mrs Emily Andrews as we should properly call her, was Grandma. She had a completely different temperament, as Valerie explained.

'Gran was an absolute sweetie. She was very kind-natured, hard-working and she knew her place. She had worked as a maid in some of Suffolk's smartest houses when she was a teenager and had a great deal of respect for authority.'

Kind-natured? Hard-working? Knew her place? Respect for authority? Maybe Giles took one look at Granny Andrews's character and created her exact opposite! But no one will ever know, because Giles took that secret with him to the grave.

Meanwhile Miss Pearl King of Bramford,

Ipswich, believes she knew Grandma 'many years ago'.

'I used to catch one of the Bluebird coaches to Felixstowe from 1952,' she recalled. 'Each morning, as I waited at the Rose and Crown stop on Norwich Road, I used to see an old lady dressed in a long black coat and skirt and black hat, carrying a string bag and often accompanied by a small mongrel dog. I always wished her good morning and, later, I got to talk to her when I met her as I was shopping one Saturday.

'She was quite an educated lady. She told me her name was Miss Alice Richardson and that she lived with her sister in Waterloo Lane. If this lady was not the original Grandma, then she was an excellent double,' added Miss King.

Giles's brother-in-law, Basil Wilson, who lives near Ipswich, believes that Grandma was based on Giles's mother-in-law and Joan's mother. But when pressed, Basil said he had no evidence for this – not even a mischievous hint from Giles himself.

We are now nearing the end of our tortuous journey in search of the real Grandma and, although there have been a couple of red herrings and false turns on the way, the conclusion is inescapable.

Ultimately, Grandma is a wonderful, unique amalgam of characteristics and prejudices born of Giles's vivid imagination. Some of these characteristics and many of these prejudices were shared by Giles himself.

She was often his mouthpiece, especially when the posturing of politicians or the little Hitler behaviour of pen-pushing bureaucrats became impossible to bear. She must have been very therapeutic, allowing Giles to attack his favourite targets in front of millions of adoring readers. And it was very therapeutic for us, the readers, too. We, like Giles, were often the hapless victims of the slings and arrows of outrageous petty officialdom.

It would, however, be simplistic to say that Giles was Grandma. He was too subtle a man and too clever an artist to base his main character just on one person.

Visually, Grandma came straight from the 1950s – and never changed. That made her a fascinating anachronism in the 1980s, but no one seemed to notice, let alone mind. She may have been stuck in a timewarp when it came to the fashion stakes, but that imbued her antics with added colour and eccentricity.

I suspect that Giles used Granny Andrews as a

working visual model for Grandma, without Granny Andrews ever knowing. Her distinctive dress sense, with that long black coat and bird-encrusted hat, would have struck Giles immediately. It was the perfect garb for someone like Grandma and easily recognisable in the 1950s. And, as we have seen, other elderly ladies adopted this striking dress code in the 1960s and 1970s, even though it became out of date. But that is just a suspicion, and nothing more. There may have well been other models for Grandma; it is impossible to tell.

What is clear, however, is that Grandma is one of the greatest ever characters in the illustrious history of British cartoons. Her origins may be murky – and her morals certainly are – but she bursts from the page as a multi-dimensional, utterly believable battleaxe whose outrageous behaviour kept us consistently amused for nearly half a century.

And that, ultimately, is all that matters.

Chapter Six

Grandma, we love you ... the tributes pour in

It is surprising that someone who was overtly prejudiced, morally dubious and doggedly self-indulgent has such a special place in our affections. But Grandma does. And how.

In simple terms, her popularity springs from her highly developed sense of humour and her hatred of authority. We can forgive, and almost forget, her pilfering in church, her teasing of Vera and her mixture of self-aggrandisement and self-delusion. These pale into insignificance when compared with her joyfully oblique look at the world and her spot-on attacks on pig-headed officials who made her life – and make our lives – a misery.

Both these enduring qualities struck a deep chord with the British people when Grandma first burst on to the scene in the 1950s. It is significant that she is as popular now as she was then and, as we shall see, this popularity spanned the political, social and intellectual divide.

In 1960, Colin MacInnes wrote in the *New Left Review*: 'Grandma is, above all, a performer. A survival from the distant music hall era, she embodies the robust virtues (and appalling nuisance value) of the vanished, or vanishing, working-class matriarch.'

The key words here are 'nuisance value'. By 1960, Grandma had already become a national institution *because* she caused a nuisance – and she tended to cause a nuisance to those who most deserved it. Incidentally, it is reassuring to find that MacInnes, who was so wrong about Giles's politics (see

Chapter 1), was at least right about Grandma in this respect.

But he cannot have looked too closely at Grandma. One of Giles's greatest joys was to set up figures of authority so that Grandma could knock them down again.

This point was well made in the *Independent*'s thoughtful obituary of Giles, arguably the most sensitive and informed tributes to the cartoonist on his death. It stated:

> *Black-coated, black-hearted and squat, she wasn't choosy in her malevolence . . . She was heroic and, as a hero, she was much needed. The Britannia of Tenniel and Partridge hardly suited a nation whose potential to cut ice in the world was sadly diminished, but Grandma as Britannia was just right. She might be old and steeped in sin, but she never knew when the game was up. Brandishing her parrot-head umbrella, she would have whacked our lads inland on the beaches of Dunkirk and prodded them upwards on to the summit of Everest.*

Meanwhile, Giles Junior, a perceptive critic of both Grandma and Giles Senior, seconded this assessment in one of his many amusing, scrawled letters. 'If Grandma had burned her bra,' he wrote, 'it would have gone up like Vesuvius.'

Joan Collins, a great fan, believed that Grandma would have been a superb addition to that tremendously popular American soap opera, *Dynasty*, in which Joan played queen bitch, Alexis Carrington.

In her introduction to the *Giles Annual* of 1986, she wrote: 'I have always giggled at Grandma. I often feel that the only character who could ever get the better of Alexis would be Grandma. Now there's an idea for a cartoon. Oh Grandma, we'd love to have you in it.'

Comedian Eric Morecambe, a self-confessed Giles addict, was equally fulsome in his praise.

'Giles is a genius,' he wrote. 'My favourite character is Grandma. Is she any relation to Ernie Wise? They are built along similar lines and Ern carries the same type of handbag. I love the way she always has Basil Brush slung around her neck when she's out terrorising the local neighbourhood.'

Radio and television comedy writer, Denis Norden, believed that Grandma 'was the only credible figure left in public life' in 1979.

Actress Joanna Lumley was typically effusive and gushing: 'Grandma is immortal . . . with her mouth snapped shut like a turtle and coal-sack body clutching a padlocked handbag.'

If there was ever a glamorous granny competition between the lovely Miss Lumley and Grandma, I know that I'd be pretty safe putting my money on Grandma. She'd have bribed – or threatened – the judges, of course, but she would also have genuinely believed that she had the edge over Miss Lumley when it came to looks.

Grandma would also have had her own say in the debate about the nation's favourite grandmother. The Queen Mother has collected a lot of votes over the years, with her dignity and her charm (two concepts alien to Grandma), but I don't think the Queen Mum would have had it all her way.

Journalist Jane Jakeman, who grew up in the 1950s, found Grandma a refreshing antithesis from the Queen Mother.

'If the Queen Mother was the fairy godmother, then Giles's Grandma was the wicked witch. Grandma wore funereal black from head to toe whereas the Queen Mother was always presented as an airy powder-puff of pastels,' Ms Jakeman wrote in the *Independent* when Giles died.

'Grandma had a permanent expression of bad temper, the Queen Mother had a perpetual gracious smile as she waved from balcony or carriage. And, as the Queen Mother aged gracefully, Grandma changed horribly into wrinkles and tantrums,' added Ms Jakeman.

I'm not entirely sure that Grandma would have approved of this rather back-handed compliment. Words like 'wrinkles' and 'tantrums' might have had her reaching for her umbrella and applying its knobbed handle to young Jane's backside.

Giles's views towards his most famous creation were clearly ambivalent and, as we shall see in Chapter 7, he even contemplated killing her off. But the outcry from Grandma's multitude of devoted fans was such that he had to abandon the idea at once. Like Frankenstein – and just as pretty – Grandma had outwitted her maker.

Eventually even Giles had to accept that Grandma was immortal – and that was the best tribute the old battleaxe could ever have wished for.

Chapter Seven

Everything you wanted to know about Grandma and were too afraid to ask . . .

The origins of Grandma are murky on two counts. First of all, no one is quite sure exactly when and where she first emerged into an unsuspecting world. Secondly, her immediate family were pretty dubious types. Cousin Norris, for example, ended up with a hangman's rope around his neck.

The demise of poor Norris, a jockey, gives us a clue about Grandma's age. We know he died in 1902 aged, I would say, about thirty. If we assume that Grandma and Norris were contemporaries, as cousins are wont to be, then they would both have been born circa 1870.

We also know that Grandma's mother once washed up at a fête attended by Queen Victoria – or at least Grandma claimed she did – thanks to a cartoon dated 24 September 1985. That tallies with our timescale.

To my mind, Grandma first appeared as Grandma in a Giles cartoon in 1945 on the railway track (I'm ignoring that rather pale, smiling imitation of Grandma in *Reynolds News* in 1940), looking about eighty. In 1953 Giles was more specific. In a perceptive article entitled *Which Is The Tiresome Age?*, he let slip that Grandma was eighty-seven. She was born, therefore, in 1866.

In 1866 Queen Victoria, a role model for

"The fact that your mother helped wash-up at a fete attended by Queen Victoria hardly qualifies you to write 12 volumes on the lives of the entire Royal Family."

Daily Express, September 24th, 1985

"SHE'S SEVEN – she simply won't do what she's told."

"SHE'S 17 – she's always in tears over some man."

"SHE'S 27 – she thinks she's a fund of experience."

"SHE'S 37 – she talks of nothing but the children."

"SHE'S 47 – she simply won't grow old gracefully."

"SHE'S 57 – she insists she's lonely and unwanted."

"SHE'S 77 – she growls at our guests."

"SHE'S 87 – she simply won't do what she's told."

Daily Express, December 28th, 1953

Grandma, was well into her lengthy reign and Britain ruled the empire and the waves. The Education Act, which established the principle of free education for all, was about to be passed – and clearly passed Grandma by.

There is the problem that Grandma would then have been 120 years old when she allowed Butch to slip his lead and canter off down the Channel Tunnel to France, but I think we can draw a discreet veil over that.

Where was she born? Well, it's possible that she's a northern lass. From time to time we hear about Grandma's northern sisters – and they even appear in one memorable cartoon (2 December 1963), frightening the hell out of the rest of the family during a holiday in Blackpool. They are identical to Grandma in every respect save one. They aren't carrying umbrellas.

Clearly, Grandma had a great time with her sisters because two days later she complained when the Family wanted to move on to other great northern towns such as Hebden Bridge, Burnley, Dewsbury and Wakefield. She just wanted to stay in Blackpool with her sisters (or aunty grandmas, as Giles Junior liked to call them).

She also had a 'wee sister' in Aberdeen, which gave her the excuse to play *Scotland the Brave* all the way through breakfast on the occasion of the return of the Scottish World Cup football team (25 June 1974). This followed one of Scotland's less ignominious displays abroad. There were other sisters called Millie, whom we meet face-downwards on an express train (20 September 1981), Florrie, who apparently lived in France (19 August 1980) and Ivy, who was mentioned fleetingly in a 1964 cartoon.

Was Grandma Scottish, then? Or from Blackpool? The clues are few and far between.

So it is probably time to employ a little piece of Giles-esque licence. If we assume that Grandma was either working, or lower-middle, class, then it is more than likely that she came from either one of Scotland's two great cities Edinburgh or Glasgow or England's Liverpool or Manchester.

We know that Grandma's father was a military man, albeit a rather spineless-looking one. Her mother, meanwhile, has a hint of those airs and graces that would have been summarily knocked out of her in Glasgow or in Manchester.

Both Edinburgh and Liverpool, though, have fine military traditions and, crucially, they have splendid racecourses. Grandma was seen at Aintree

"Stand by for a fab bout of Blackpool hospitality, daddyo – here come two of Grandma's northern sisters."

Daily Express, December 2nd, 1963

"Dad, why do we have to have 'Scotland the Brave' all through breakfast just because Grandma's got a wee sister in Aberdeen?"

Daily Express, June 25th, 1974

"What special rights has Roy Jenkins got to stop the non-stop London Express that my sister Millie hasn't got?"

Sunday Express, September 20th, 1981

"She says we made Dunkirk in 1940, so we can make it again to pick up her sister, Florrie."

Daily Express, August 19th, 1980

as early as 1952 and it could just be that she was returning home.

Either way, the racecourse may have been where Grandma spent the majority of her schooldays because there is no evidence that she ever went to school. She always had a certain amount of native wit and cunning, but her extraordinary words and deeds over the years never betrayed the slightest hint of learning.

At some stage Grandma must have got married. It's a strange thought, I know, imagining her walking down the aisle with some hen-pecked husband. (Well, he had to be henpecked, didn't he? If he had given as good as he presumably got, then the marital home would have resembled a particularly bloody battlefield.)

Inevitably, he did not last the pace – and he does not feature in Giles's family cartoons. Divorce? Death? Either would have seemed preferable to life with Grandma. But this shadowy figure did provide Grandma with a son and heir (we will not discuss the intricate details of this process on the grounds of decency) in Father, the titular head of the family.

From 1945 onwards, Grandma seemed perfectly happy in her matriarchal role, cutting a colourful

"You and your 'Let's sit under that hedge out of the wind'."

Daily Express, April 7th, 1952

127

"If I were you, Vera, I'd get Mr Bush and Saddam Hussein to split the bill."

Daily Express, 1990

figure as she stomped through life in her own inimitable way and at her own measured pace. She certainly never mentioned her own marriage – and no man ever dared to suggest the possibility of her marrying again. She might have taken them up on it.

She lived in domestic chaos in a comparatively spacious suburban house. One cannot be more specific than that, though it would be nice to think it was in Ipswich. Now and again, much to Grandma's annoyance, she was carted off on holiday to foreign climes (21 June 1961 and 20 October 1963). Money does not appear to have been a burning issue because, even though Grandma was always complaining that she did not have enough, she never wanted for the basic necessities of life like beer and fags.

Her closest relationship was with Vera, closely followed by Butch the dog, her cigarettes, her bookmaker, Ipswich Town FC and her bottles of brown ale and whisky.

Some of Giles's funniest cartoons feature Grandma, Vera and the doctor's surgery. Vera, the hypochondriac par excellence, treated the surgery – and the pharmacy – as a second home and Grandma liked to accompany her there, just to fire off a volley of salacious and suggestive comments in the direction of the doctor.

Harassed GPs were accused of trying to proposition Vera and hypnotise her for (heaven forbid) sexual gratification (6 March 1988), while pharmacists could only marvel at the amount of pills Vera was able to consume.

On one occasion, as Vera struggled out of Timothy Boots (a typical Giles amalgam of Timothy Whites and Boots) with a sack load of pills, Grandma's face creased into one of those wonderfully mischievous smiles as she cracked: 'If I were you, Vera, I'd get Mr Bush and Saddam Hussein to split the bill.' This was, of course, at the height of the Gulf War.

This was one of Grandma's last jokes because her creator was getting increasingly old and infirm by the early 1990s. That fate never befell Grandma and she looked just as sprightly in Timothy Boots – if not more so – as she did on that deserted railway line nearly half a century previously.

I suspect that Giles would have been rather miffed that Grandma outlived him, especially since he had tried to kill her off on more than one occasion. But Grandma was not to be defeated.

Peter Tory, Giles's official biographer, was aghast

"Who wrote to Lord Matthews and nominated me for first of the chops?"

Sunday Express, July 27th, 1980

at the prospect of Grandma's demise, writing: 'What would the funeral itself have been like? One can only speculate. Perhaps, like her hero Churchill, she would have made her last journey downriver on a magnificent barge . . . the Queen would have worn black.'

It was not to be. Every time Grandma was left out of the cartoons for more than a fortnight, her fans used to write to Giles to inquire solicitously about her health. They refused to let her die, even when Giles dropped the broadest of hints by tying Grandma to a railway line on the front of the 1990 annual or, ten years earlier, suggesting that she was 'for the chop.'

Giles claimed to be mystified by Grandma's popularity. 'You don't even see any Grandmas today,' he said towards the end of the 1980s. 'All the modern grandmas are young and glamorous like Sophia Loren.' Giles knew only too well, however, that his Grandma appealed to the young – because she was so young at heart herself.

That's not bad, really, for a 129-year-old.

Potted biography

c.1866 Born, when Lord John Russell was Prime Minister

1902 Cousin Norris, a jockey, hanged

1945 First appears in a Giles cartoon in the *Daily Express*

1956 Calls for universal hanging

1969 Visits the Isle of Wight pop festival

1978 Celebrates Ipswich Town's FA Cup win against Arsenal

1989 Offers her services at the House of Commons

1990 Is tied to a railway line by Giles

1995 Giles dies with Grandma 129 not out

Chapter Eight

Giles, Grandma and Suffolk

Grandma may not have come from Suffolk, as we have seen in the previous chapter, but she almost certainly ended up there. And, since she was such an ardent fan of Ipswich Town, what better place could there possibly be to spend the rest of her days than the centre of Ipswich itself?

There she is, in all her glory, standing proudly at the junction of Queen and Princes Streets, opposite the office-cum-studio of her creator in Butter Market. Her umbrella, held closely to her chest, is ready to smite any traffic warden or local government official who might have the temerity to come too close.

The man entrusted to immortalise Grandma in bronze was Ipswich sculptor, Miles Robinson. He was approached by the Ipswich Promotion Bureau in 1993 to design and construct the Giles Family

sculpture to celebrate Giles's fiftieth anniversary at Express Newspapers.

Robinson was honoured and only too happy to oblige. His idea was to depict Grandma with Vera, the twins and Butch the dog, but Giles was less than happy with the portrayal of Butch and asked Robinson to remove him. Alas, it was too late. Butch was already set in bronze! Giles, apparently, was furious. He called the sculptor and raged: 'The feeling seems to be that you had better leave Butch in. But I still think it's bloody awful.'

The sculpture was finally unveiled in September 1993 by comedian Warren Mitchell, in the presence of Giles and Johnny Speight. No doubt they all wet Grandma's head, metaphorically at least, with copious amounts of booze and forgot about poor old Butch – for a day or so, at least.

Whatever Giles might have thought, Miles Robinson's sculpture is an extremely popular landmark and a tribute to the town's most famous Grandma. Grandma would have loved it.

Interestingly enough, the cartoonist Holly – who worked for the Ipswich *Evening Star* and was a friend of Giles – drew a wonderful cartoon with a beaming Grandma dreaming of her very own statue in the middle of Ipswich. That was one of Grandma's dreams which came true, bless her.

It seems rather strange, given the respect and esteem in which Carl Giles is held in Ipswich and in Suffolk, that there isn't a Giles museum or a Giles trail. Either would prove extremely popular. According to tourism guides, the local council is not committed to building either. Giles would find that highly amusing, given his own views on local councils and petty bureaucrats!

In Ipswich, the tour could start with Grandma in the town centre. It's a mere stone's throw from Grandma to Giles's office. It was here that he travelled the few miles from his Witnesham farm three days a week to chronicle the latest adventures of the Family for the *Daily* and *Sunday Express*. Once they were finished, the cartoons would be dispatched to Ipswich Station by taxi and would be collected at Liverpool Street by an Express lackey. Woe betide any sub-editor who tried to change them.

When Giles had completed his day's work, and that could take anything up to four or five hours because of his attention to detail, it was time for a restorative and refreshing drink. It is at this stage that the Giles Trail might degenerate into a pub crawl, but no true Giles or Grandma fan would mind that, would they?

The cartoonist's favourite watering-hole during the day was the Centre Spot Restaurant at Portman Road, the home of Ipswich Town Football Club. Giles enjoyed his football – and was tremendous friends with the legendary Cobbolds, who ran the club – but he was ultimately there for the conversation and the beer rather than the football.

Grandma, though, would leap out of the woodwork when Ipswich Town were doing well and one of the happiest days of her life came when her team beat Arsenal in the 1978 Cup Final. Giles's cartoon depicting this joyous moment hangs proudly by the club's boardroom.

After several lagers and a couple of shorts, perhaps in the company of Johnnie Speight, Eric Sykes, Jean Rook or Tommy Cooper, Giles might well embark on a pub crawl and it is here that the Giles Trail might become a little hazy. But the trail should end at the legendary gentleman's club, The Chevallier, where Giles liked to drink and gamble until it was time to go home to his devoted and, it has to be said, long-suffering wife, Joan.

That's the town trail. The country trail might just be a little healthier. For a taste of what it might entail, it is worth going back to 1950 when Giles, in a rare moment, told readers a little bit about himself.

Son of a Newmarket racing family. Keeps horses himself. Born while parents were staying within one mile of Bow Bells, making him officially a Cockney. Schooled all over the place, but never at art school. Reached dizzy heights of working for Alexander Korda and then decided he's had enough of films. Migrated to work in riding schools and goodness knows what else.

LIKES: Farming; riding; drinking; Benjamin Britten's music; cars, engineering; drawing; people who congratulate him on cartoons which he didn't do; drinking (again).

DISLIKES: Cinema organists who are forever telling him they are going to play an old favourite which never is an old favourite by any means; and ever so many other things.

HABITS: Calls all policemen and editors 'Sir' and avoids all children under the age of thirty. Somerset House knows the rest.

Farming, riding, engineering, drawing and drinking. Those, together with sailing which later became a passion, were Giles's country pursuits. And it is these pursuits which should form the basis of any Giles country trail, especially sailing and drinking. Grandma, of course, was a great sailor and drinker too – it was just unfortunate that both these hobbies seemed to land her into an awful lot of trouble.

The country trail should start at Giles's Hillbrow Farm at Witnesham, some three miles north of Ipswich, which he bought after the Second World War to escape from the hurly-burly of London life. Hillbrow Farm was the perfect base for Giles and he was forced to admit that 'there is nothing I can complain about or dislike in Witnesham. Everyone is so friendly.' The only blot on the landscape, and they were literally blots, were the electricity pylons plonked next door to Giles's lovely house by some insensitive planners in the 1960s. Giles fought and fought them – but eventually lost, only increasing his hatred of petty officialdom.

Giles's lasting memorial to the village, apart from filling the coffers of the Barley Mow public house, was the village sign which he designed and unveiled. The sketches on which the sign is based now hang in the village hall.

Giles may have enjoyed a pint or three at the Barley Mow, but he positively loved the Maybush at Woldringfield, near Woodbridge on the River Deben. It was there that he moored his boat. The Maybush also provided the backdrop to one of his finest-ever cartoons (20 July 1952) in which the whole of Suffolk appeared to have decamped outside. The caption, quoting John Masefield, read simply: 'I must go down to the sea again, the lonely sea and sky.'

Marjorie Broughall, the former landlady of the Maybush, adored Carl Giles. 'He was the most wonderful man, extremely funny and always excellent company. He did so many drawings for us, which decorated the pub walls, and we had some exceptionally happy times together.'

One of these drawings was of Giles staring into a shaving mirror – only to find Grandma staring back!

'I wish we'd kept that one in a way, because everyone is always wondering who Grandma was based on and this suggested Giles and Grandma were one and the same. Sadly it was sold at Christies a few years ago, so it has now disappeared from public view,' she added. 'I didn't know how seriously to take that cartoon, though, because Giles was always such a joker.'

In view of his strong sailing connection, it is appropriate that both Giles and Grandma should have been honoured in 1998 by the Felixstowe Ferry Sailing Club, making this famous Ipswich

"I must go down to the sea again, to the lonely sea and the sky..."

Sunday Express, July 20th, 1952

port a new, but crucial, part of the Giles country trail.

On Sunday 23 May a support and rescue boat called Grandma (ironically, it was usually Grandma who needed supporting and rescuing) was launched at Felixstowe in memory of Giles, who was president of the club for the last ten years of his life.

Significantly, when Giles took over as the club's president, he drew a cartoon of Grandma at the top of Nelson's Column with the caption 'Under New Management'. Once again Giles was playfully blurring the lines between himself and his most famous creation.

Cars were Carl Giles's other favourite form of transport. He called himself a Bentley-driving socialist (anticipating New Labour by at least a generation) and had a selection of splendid vehicles which he drove at tremendously fast speeds around the narrow country roads. This led to numerous brushes with the law, including a refusal to take a breath test, as a cursory glance through the cuttings library at the Ipswich *Evening Star* will testify.

Giles, though, was usually very considerate to those who were unfortunate enough to encounter

The support and rescue boat Grandma *launched at Felixstowe in May 1999 (Simon Parker)*

him in Stirling Moss mode. On one occasion, having swerved to avoid two young children called Sylvia and Johnny Langley on their way to school near Witnesham, he ploughed headlong into a bus. He was so contrite that he wrote a lovely letter, with a cartoon, to the Langley family who remain – not surprisingly – among his greatest fans today.

Unlike many car enthusiasts, however, he wasn't precious about his cars. He once drove a brand-new Jaguar into a gatepost at Hillbrow Farm in order to avoid his geese!

It would be advisable to adopt a rather more

To Sylvia & Johnny.
With best wishes.
from GILES

"TWO LOVELY BLACK EYES"

Witnesham 239.

Hillbrow Farm
Witnesham
Suffolk

October 9th, 1960.

Dear Mr & Mrs Chatfield,

I do hope Sylvia and Johnny didn't get too much of a shock last Wednesday. Although the accident happened while swerving to avoid them, I would like you to know that they were in no way to blame. They were walking just as no doubt you have trained them - well into the side of the road facing oncoming traffic. It was unfortunate that at the point where I was half round the curve the overgrown hedge concealed them. I thank God that when they did step into view I was able to avoid them, even though it meant steering into the path of the oncoming bus. Fortunately the driver was travelling at a very moderate speed and the damage was not nearly as bad as it looked. In fact if the road had not been wet there wouldn't have been a collision.

Sylvia was very sweet. When I asked her if she would walk along to see Mr. Cranmer with me she was very worried as she thought it might make her late for school!

Knowing of your recent sad loss I am more relieved than ever that not even the slightest harm came to them.

Yours very sincerely,
C.R.Giles.

circumspect attitude towards driving than Giles during our country trail, although it would be more advisable still to leave the car altogether because a true Giles Trail would slowly degenerate into a full-blown pub crawl. Just about every rural hostelry within a 10-mile radius of Ipswich has a raucous Giles story to tell.

Carl Giles, however, was cosmopolitan in his tastes and his friends and he enjoyed a very close relationship with Johnny and Patrick Cobbold, the two patrician brothers who ran Ipswich Town FC and preferred sophisticated restaurants and smart hotels to rural inns. The multi-starred Maison Tolbooth at Dedham was an especial favourite. Two original Giles cartoons hang proudly in the gunroom-cum-lavatory of Glemham Hall, the elegant Cobbold family seat near Woodbridge. The choice of room would have appealed to Grandma's earthy sense of humour.

The rural trail should end where it began at Hillbrow Farm, where Carl Giles found so much peace, tranquillity and inspiration away from the madding world with his pigs, his cars, his gadgets and, above all, his wife Joan.

Joan, with her gentle, tolerant and measured view of life, was the exact antithesis of Grandma.

Chapter Nine

Grandma in the modern world

One of the great characteristics of Grandma was that she always seemed at home – wherever she was. Whether she was studying the form of horses as they were out on the gallops in 1950 or inspecting the embryonic Channel Tunnel forty years later, Grandma seemed to fit, even if she might appear to others to be an anachronistic old witch.

She survived the Swinging Sixties and the Thatcherite Eighties, both testing decades in their different ways, with consummate ease and she was limbering up to take the 1990s by storm when her creator fell ill and died.

So how would Grandma have fared today in the touchy-feely world of Tony Blair's New Labour and the encroaching powers of Europe? What would she have felt about the promiscuous behaviour of President of the United States, Bill Clinton? The war in Kosovo? Gay clergymen? Sky TV? Computers? And London's Millennium Dome? We can only hazard a guess – but one thing is for sure, she would have had a view on each and every one of these subjects.

There are various aspects of life in the 1990s of which she would have approved. The long-overdue legislation which ushered in all-day and all-night drinking would have received a resounding thumbs up, as would the vastly improved coverage of horse-racing on television. Elsewhere, sadly, Grandma would have found precious little to cheer about.

The changing role of the grandmother within the

family would have given her particular unease. In the 1940s and 1950s, the British grandmother, like her European counterparts, was regarded as a crucial part of the family. That is why the Family never questioned Grandma's right to be in their midst, however infuriating she might have been. That certainly isn't the case these days. Residential and nursing homes for the elderly have sprung up all over the country during the past twenty-five years, assuming the responsibility for looking after the elderly. Had anyone had the temerity, or the stupidity, to suggest that Grandma should move into such a home, they would have felt the full force of her tongue – and her umbrella.

The United Nations has designated 1999 as the Year of the Elderly. This worthwhile initiative has prompted Paul Gravett, the curator of the Cartoon Art Trust Gallery off Russell Square in London, to hold a special exhibition featuring Grandma in the autumn. She would have been tickled pink.

'Grandma is a perfect symbol for the older person. She is vigorous, opinionated, in control (most of the time) and funny. Despite her faults, I think she is someone to aspire to, she's a role model,' commented Paul Gravett. 'It makes perfect sense to celebrate the Year of the Elderly with a collection of the very best Grandma cartoons. She lives on in so many people's memories and it will be great to have another look at her anti-authoritarian view of life,' he added. 'I am sure that this exhibition will prove to be one of the most popular – if not *the* most popular – we have held this year.'

The London-based Cartoon Art Trust is a great supporter of Carl Giles. In 1993 the Trust held a superb retrospective of Giles's work to celebrate his fifty years at the *Daily Express*. This exhibition

Dennis Main Wilson (right), English humourist, with Paul Gravett at the 1993 exhibition at the Cartoon Art Trust

"If the French don't want our lamb why don't we tell them we won't let them have any?"

underlined the cartoonist's pivotal place in the history of twentieth-century British drawing and art.

They would also have had tremendous fun with the ludicrous European directives about the shape of bananas and the like, while the behaviour of the corrupt European Commission, whose members resigned en masse before reappointing themselves, would have given Grandma apoplexy. There's no doubt that Jacques Santer and his fellow commission members would have felt the full force of Grandma's anger in their cosy Brussels headquarters. They would have been lucky had they lived to tell the tale.

How Grandma would have reacted to the sexual antics of US President Bill Clinton would have been a different matter altogether. Power was something of an aphrodisiac to Grandma (she once turned up at the House of Commons in the hope of getting a job as a call girl) and Clinton's shenanigans in the Oval Office of the White House would not have put Grandma off at all. Quite the opposite, in fact. She could well have given him an encouraging telephone call of support at the height of the impeachment crisis – although I doubt that the idea of phone sex would have appealed.

Neither, I suspect, would the Millennium Dome. Grandma would have been furious at the amount of money wasted on what she would have regarded as a useless monstrosity. Could it not have been better spent on increasing her pension? Or slashing the taxes on whisky, beer and betting? Or cutting prescription charges, so that Vera might be able to afford to buy herself a new outfit?

Grandma would also have disliked the increasingly impersonal and computerised nature of our society today. She loved the face-to-face confrontation, the sound of the whack of her umbrella on a gas board official's head, a crunch of a fist in a planning official's face and the thud of her padlocked handbag on her bank manager's desk. She loved inspiring fear and loathing amongst petty officials and pen-pushing bureaucrats. It was her very therapeutic form of revenge.

But would Grandma have enjoyed today's television programmes? Her favourites like *Morecame and Wise* and *Mike Yarwood* have long since gone, to be replaced by numerous vulgar and unfunny acts whose comedy is – shall we say – an acquired taste. No, I suspect she would have been tuned permanently to Channel 4 Racing, Wimbledon (although she never really recovered from the

"Don't let 'em soften you up, Mac – get in there and give the umpires hell."

Daily Express, June 21st, 1988

"Hold tight Gascoigne, she's had enough of Gazzamania."

retirement of John McEnroe) and, just possibly, *Countdown*. She always fancied herself as an intellectual! *Songs Of Praise* would be no good, though, because Grandma wouldn't be able to pinch the collection.

Finally, Grandma would have been appalled by the cult of the dim-witted entertainer as God. She had already expressed her dislike of Gazzamania in 1990, when this cult was in its infancy, and it has got progressively worse since. For Gazza, read Shazza, Bazza, Dazza and countless other yobs and tartlets who have hit the jackpot in the media merry-go-round. Grandma would have treated them all with the same icy disdain reserved for gas board and tax officials.

The political, social, economic and intellectual climate has changed radically since Grandma first stormed on to the pages of the *Daily Express* nearly sixty years ago. But she has remained steadfast in her likes and her dislikes, her hopes and her fears, her prejudices and, well, her extreme prejudices. Like her statue in the middle of Ipswich, she is a reassuring port in the middle of a violent storm.

So, when everything is considered, Grandma would have felt at home today – just as she always did. The world, you see, is still as absurd as ever.

Chapter Ten

Farewell to Grandma with six of the best

The highlight of many people's Christmas during Giles's heyday was finding his latest annual peeping out of the stocking or nestling under the Christmas tree. The new annual was as much part of the festive season as the Queen's speech, Christmas pudding and falling asleep on the sofa in front of the television.

Part of the fascination of the new Giles annual was discovering which famous person had been asked to write the introduction that year. Giles used to take a special interest in this and would often approach celebrities themselves to see if they would do the honours. They rarely refused.

These introductions are now fascinating period pieces, transporting us back to those heady days when media stars like Terry Wogan and Mike Yarwood bestrode the earth. Some are excellent, notably Michael Parkinson's perceptive piece in 1973, and some are terrible. Angela Rippon's offering, in which she unforgivably refers to Grandma as gran, and other members of the family as baby and junior, was unfortunately a little disappointing.

My favourite introduction was by Sir Alistair Burnet, the ITN newscaster and, more importantly, Giles's editor at the *Daily Express*. I think it is worth quoting Sir Alastair at length because, despite the flowery language, his comments capture the essence of Giles and Gilesland. In the foreward to the 1984 annual, he wrote:

It is a country wholly surrounded by choppy seas and duffers in boats. Its pastures are peopled by idle cattle, idle farm hands and even idler earls. No snow falls there which does not end up impacting on the necks of vicars and postmen. No rain falls that does not raise the grass for the lawnmower industry.

It is not a democracy but an anarchy, the urban guerrillas led by a gerontic Passionara in black. Its pubs never close, its butlers never falter. Its men are pitiable but persevering, its women patient in their superiority, its children numerous. It is full of mischief. We have to shout on News At Ten *to make ourselves heard above the Gilesland hubbub.*

A gerontic Passionara in black? Well, Grandma has been called many things in her time, but this was definitely a first. I suspect she would have been rather flattered with the description, because it sounds vaguely aggressive and very important, even though she, like everyone else, would not have had the faintest clue what it meant.

The point that Sir Alastair made, however, is a sound one. Gilesland is a wonderful, chaotic and hilarious place where the matriarchal Grandma holds sway – courtesy of her umbrella, her wit and her sheer cussedness. She evolved from the disgruntled old lady on a railway track in 1945 to a treasured national institution fifty years later when her creator died.

It was a perfectly natural evolution and it is worth tracing this evolution with the help of six of Giles's greatest Grandma cartoons before we bid both Giles and Grandma a fond farewell. All these cartoons are perfect examples of Giles's consummate draughtsmanship, his mastery of movement and detail, his eye for the absurd, his unique wit and, above all, his love of Grandma.

The first cartoon is a classic of its kind. It was drawn in September 1960 when Giles and Grandma were both getting firmly into their stride. Grandma has just been told that there was a 100-year-old 'Grandma-artist' in America who only started painting when she was 77. Her fertile imagination gives her an idea.

With paint brush in mouth and palette at hand, she persuades mother and father to sit for a Renaissance-style portrait which involves mother posing as Cupid and aiming a bow and arrow in a general direction of her disgruntled-looking

"That was a bright stroke telling Grandma there is a famous Grandma-artist in America who is 100 years old and didn't take up painting till she was 77."

Daily Express, September 6th, 1960

"Mum! Grandma's gone down behind the piano."

Daily Express, December 28th, 1974

husband. Vera, meanwhile, is having trouble standing still and Ernie is gazing at the heavens in despair. Elsewhere, the detail is amazing, but the lasting impression is of Grandma having a tremendous time – at everyone else's expense. How that theme was to echo down the years.

Moving swiftly forward to Christmas 1974 and a cartoon of classic simplicity. Clearly, one of the family's Christmas presents that year was a trampoline – and Grandma, no doubt buoyed up by excess Christmas cheer, could not wait to try it out. Oh dear! One jump, and she's been catapulted behind the piano.

Apart from being extremely funny (a single joke is often the most effective), this cartoon is an excellent example of Giles's mastery of movement which he learned and perfected when he worked as an animator for Alexander Korda in the 1930s. He has captured the bounce of the trampoline so well. Oh yes, and do look at mother's face, half-horrified and half-resigned, in the background.

The next cartoon, which appeared just under one year later, plays upon the highly amusing relationship between Ernie and Grandma. Ernie takes great delight in ridiculing Grandma, but only behind her back or when she is asleep. (He's no fool!) On this occasion she is asleep, handcuffed to her padlocked handbag, when the news comes through that the Loch Ness monster has made one of its periodic appearances.

In a flash Ernie is on the telephone, ringing up the Natural History Museum, saying: 'We have photographic proof of another monster – colour mostly black, fur around neck, powerful flippers…' Meanwhile, if you look carefully, there's a tiny effigy of Grandma in the right-hand corner of the cartoon, underlining Giles's love of inserting understated little gems to be discovered by the discerning fan.

We all know Grandma loves a drink and that is one of her most endearing qualities. Giles has made capital out of her drinking habits in a cartoon published on 26 September 1982 which is very funny – and also has a moral.

A policeman has arrived at the chaotic family home (two hoovers are on the go, bottles are popping and Butch looks as though he has just finished a very raucous bout of barking) with some disturbing news. He has a summons from a burglar who broke in and stole half a bottle of Grandma's homemade wine. Apparently, according to the policeman, the burglar has never been the same since.

"It's a summons from a burglar who broke in and stole half a bottle of Grandma's home-made wine and has never been the same since."

Sunday Express, September 26th, 1982

"I can see the headline, Vera – 'Amorous GP tells sexy patient to take her hat off.'"

Sunday Express, March 6th, 1988

In the background, we can see Grandma hard at work treading the grapes (look carefully and there is a tantalising glimpse of her feet and ankles) with Natalie the cat stretched out on her back, snoring and very, very drunk. Clearly, she has imbibed some of Grandma's lethal wine. Meanwhile, one can almost hear the resounding cheer from Middle England, sickened by the relentless tide of crime, celebrating the news that Grandma has laid a member of the criminal fraternity low.

Grandma seems to come into her own when she accompanies the snivelling Vera in the doctor's surgery. Perhaps inspired by the sheer range of Vera's ailments, and relieved that she does not suffer from any of them herself, Grandma is often at her funniest in the waiting room as her wicked, surreal sense of humour moves into overdrive. She usually manages to insult both the doctor and Vera with one cutting comment and this is precisely the case in the fifth classic cartoon, published in the *Sunday Express* on 6 March 1988.

The waiting room is full of a gruesome collection of hypochondriacs and spot-infested children, but Grandma – head deep inside a newspaper – is oblivious. She is much keener on a story in her paper concerning the tape-recording of a naked GP's surgery sex romps, which she recounts to Vera with glee: 'I can see the headline, Vera – Amorous GP tells sexy patient to take her hat off.' Poor Vera, holding her baby, looks suitably appalled.

Finally it is reassuring to report that Grandma sometimes met her match. She did on 4 June 1989 – at the hands of an African elephant! As Grandma is giving the elephant one of her quizzical stares, the animal uncoils its trunk and unleashes a torrent of water all over Grandma. She is totally soaked, while Vera's glasses are knocked for six. And what was the elephant's problem? The handle of Grandma's trusty umbrella, the scourge of so many who crossed Grandma's path, was made of ivory.

There are those who believed that Giles's powers were on the wane as the 1980s drew to a close, including – ominously – the then editor of the *Daily Express*, Sir Nicholas Lloyd. But this hilarious send-up of Grandma proves that there was life in the old cartoonist yet, even though he was battling against increasing ill health.

The relationship between Sir Nicholas and Giles was certainly not made in heaven. Sir Nicholas, unlike so many previous editors, did not value Giles's work and in 1989 the cartoonist parted

"I bet she didn't know her umbrella handle was made of ivory."

Sunday Express, June 4th, 1989

company with his beloved *Express* after forty-seven years, saying bluntly after yet another row with his editor: 'I just thought, sod this.' Posterity will judge whether Sir Nicholas was right or wrong.

In many ways, it already has. Carl Giles is now regarded as the most popular British cartoonist of the twentieth century – with Grandma as his most enduring creation. There are many reasons for Giles's popularity. He was a brilliant draughtsman, with an unerring eye and memory for detail which he likened to a 'disease'. He was also exceptionally funny and created a family which cut across the political and social boundaries of Britain and spoke directly to you and me. He was an uncommon man, with the common touch.

Grandma, meanwhile, was a most uncommon woman with a touch which could reduce grown men to tears, especially if they were gas board officials, door-to-door salesmen, local authority bureaucrats or punk rockers.

Her tough, uncompromising, refreshing and sometimes madcap outlook on life still has the capacity to make us both laugh and think. We laugh with her – and at her – because she is so damn funny; and we think because, yes, Grandma was right not to put up with all the nonsense that is often foisted upon us in this strange, mixed-up world.

In that sense, Giles *was* Grandma. He, too, hated the planners who allowed a string of giant electricity pylons to be built next to his farmhouse; the health police who railed at his smoking and drinking; the real police who did not like his driving; the politicians who broke every promise they made; and the faceless, pen-pushing bureaucrats who made so many people's lives a misery.

In another sense, however, Grandma was greater than Giles. Just like Frankenstein's monster (though Grandma will not be flattered by the comparison), she became too big for her creator to handle. As we have seen, the faintest suggestion that she might be killed off caused such an outcry that Giles was forced to abandon the idea. The family without Grandma would have been like Morecame and Wise without Morecambe, or fish and chips without the chips. It would have been unthinkable.

When Grandma first impinged on the public's consciousness on that deserted railway track, she could scarcely have imagined what an amazing journey lay ahead of her – and us. It was a journey which saw her strike a blow for those free spirits everywhere who believe that life is worth living to the full and to hell with the consequences.

Hell is where many of Grandma's victims may have wished to consign her. But she was a tremendous survivor and had no intention of giving anyone the satisfaction of seeing her burn in perpetuity. In any case, she would have frightened the life out of the devil.

No, I suspect that Grandma is now enjoying her own little slice of heaven in a snug bar somewhere with a drink in one hand, a betting slip in the other, a cigarette in her mouth, a witticism on her lips and Vera by her side. And there, sitting in the same bar and gazing at her with fond approval, is Carl Giles.